THE NUTRiBULLET CLASSIC RECIPE BOOK

The NUTRiBULLET Classic RECIPE BOOK

200 Health Boosting Delicious and Nutritious Blast and Smoothie Recipes

RECIPROCITY

Third Edition published by Reciprocity in 2015
All rights reserved

WRITER	EDITOR
Susan Fotherington	**James Watkins**
NUTRITION ADVISOR	ILLUSTRATOR
Sibel Osman	**David Joyce**

Copyright © Reciprocity, London 2015
All Rights Reserved. No part of this publication may be reproduced, stored in a retrieval system, or transmitted, in any form, or by any means, electronic, mechanical, photocopying, recording or otherwise, without the prior permission of the publisher and copyright holder.

Disclaimer
The information in this book is provided on the basis that neither the authors nor the editors nor the publishers shall have any responsibility for any loss or damage that results or is claimed to have resulted from reading it. Some of the recipes contain nuts or nut milk. If you have a nut allergy please avoid those particular recipes. The NutriBullet™ is a registered trademark of Homeland Housewares, LLC. Reciprocity is not affiliated with the owner of the trademark and is not an authorized distributor of the trademark owner's products or services. This publication has not been prepared, approved or licensed by NutriBullet™ or Homeland Housewares, LLC.

THE NUTRiBULLET CLASSIC RECIPE BOOK

CONTENTS

All recipes are stated in Cups, Grams and Ounces.

*All recipes are stated in Cups, Grams and Ounces.
The precise nutritional break down into Protein grams, Fat grams, Carb grams, Fibre grams and Kcals is calculated for each recipe using data from the U.S. Department of Agriculture database.*

Health Benefits 9
Essential Amino Acids 10
Essential Vitamins 11
Essential Oils and Fats 11
Essential Minerals 11
Superfoods 12
Sleep and Foods 15
Eat a Rainbow of Colour 17
Nutrition Data 18
NutriBullet Capacities 18
Cleaning and Warnings 19
Tips and Extras 20

Superfood Smoothies
Made entirely out of Superfoods

Chard on Apricot	22
Broccoli Blockbuster	22
Blackberry and Raspberry Piazza	23
Broccoli and Avocado Fiesta	23
Spinach and Guava Boost	24
Apricot needs Raspberry	24
Broccoli goes Papaya	25

Blueberry Boost 25
Chard joins Raspberry 26
Spinach embraces Papaya 26
Chard and Blueberry Revision 27
Spinach and Apricot Therapy 27
Chard Crush 28
Black Kale in Avocado 28
Black Kale Bonanza 29
Broccoli meets Blackberry 29
Chard loves Guava 30
Spinach Sunset 30
Spinach and Blueberry Concerto 31
Black Kale in Blackberry 31

Superfood Blasts
Made entirely out of Superfoods

Black Kale goes Blueberry 32
Spinach meets Pumpkin 32
Almond Amazement 33
Guava loves Chia 33
Blackberry and Flax Elixir 34
Raspberry and Pumpkin Consortium 34
Goji Gala 35
Guava Galaxy 35
Spinach joins Raspberry 36
Avocado Adventure 36
Broccoli embraces Blueberry 37
Flax Fiesta 37
Papaya Paradise 38
Spinach needs Almond 38
Raspberry Regatta 39
Avocado on Flax 39
Blackberry Bliss 40
Goji needs Chia 40
Pumpkin Perfection 41
Broccoli and Raspberry Mist 41

Heart Care Blasts
High in Omega 3 etc.

Spinach Supermodel 42
Walnut Revision 42
Broccoli Bliss 43
Pecan Perfection 43
Spinach in Flax 44
Broccoli and Tangerine Dream 44
Flax Fusion 45
Spinach and Walnut Elixir 45
Blackberry loves Tomato 46
Lettuce embraces Chia 46
Carrot Cornucopia 47
Spinach on Blueberry 47
Rocket Mirage 48
Spinach meets Orange 48
Broccoli and Nectarine Delight 49
Red Pepper Reaction 49
Rocket and Orange Opera 50
Raspberry Recovery 50
Broccoli goes Blackberry 51
Lettuce and Guava Panacea 51

Happiness, Deep Sleep and Stress Busting Blasts
High in Tryptophan, Magnesium, Vit B3, B6, B9

Carrot Constellation 52
Watercress and Avocado Invigorator 52
Prune and Beetroot Kiss 53
Broccoli and Sunflower Garden 53
Prune Panache 54
Spinach and Cashew Cascade 54
Watercress Waistline 55
Spinach joins Avocado 55
Watercress goes Spinach 56
Broccoli embraces Peanut 56
Prune and Cauliflower Ensemble 57

Broccoli Morning ... 57
Spinach Heaven ... 58
Pumpkin Power ... 58
Apricot finds Beetroot ... 59
Chia Collection ... 59
Sunflower Blossom ... 60
Apricot Debut ... 60
Watercress and Sesame Mist ... 61
Avocado Anthem ... 61

Classic Desserts

Raspberry in Walnut ... 62
Plum and Peach Paradise ... 62
Prune Cleanser ... 63
Banana joins Pecan ... 63
Peeled Fig and Hazelnut Feast ... 64
Pear invites Almond ... 64
Strawberry Sunshine ... 65
Date Dictator ... 65
Prune meets Peanut ... 66
Blueberry and Goji Heaven ... 66
Guava on Clementine ... 67
Melon and Cashew Delivered ... 67
Orange Orchard ... 68
Kiwi embraces Brazil ... 68
Tangerine and Pineapple Piazza ... 69
Tangerine and Peanut Nexus ... 69
Kiwi goes Walnut ... 70
Papaya and Almond Seduction ... 70
Cashew Chorus ... 71
Mango joins Goji ... 71

Classic Blasts

Fennel Fiesta ... 72
Walnut Waterfall ... 72

Red Cabbage Cascade	73
Water Melon Miracle	73
Tangerine goes Raspberry	74
Green Cabbage meets Mango	74
Melon Melody	75
Watercress and Brazil Royale	75
Green Cabbage Crush	76
Rocket and Blueberry Feast	76
Broccoli embraces Peach	77
Banana loves Sesame	77
Red Grape in Apricot	78
Lettuce Lagoon	78
Watercress and Orange Revelation	79
Goji Guru	79
Cranberry Holiday	80
Kiwi finds Sesame	80
Green Cabbage joins Peeled Fig	81
Grapefruit needs Pecan	81
Nectarine on Apple	82
Rocket and Blackberry Vortex	82
Rocket Regatta	83
Guava and Hazelnut Detente	83
Peach Paradox	84
Celeriac Cascade	84
Yellow Pepper Splash	85
Guava and Hazelnut Elixir	85
Broccoli Blockbuster	86
Bok Choy and Pecan Vortex	86
Tangerine and Sesame Journey	87
Red Cabbage Rejunevator	87
Broccoli meets Walnut	88
Watercress and Cranberry Nectar	88
Water Melon and Almond Invigorator	89
Mint goes Red Grape	89
Brazil Bliss	90
Red Cabbage and Cashew Panacea	90
Rocket invites Apple	91
Red Pepper Rave	91
Mint loves Peanut	92

Watercress and Hazelnut Potion ... 92
Swede Symphony ... 93
Watercress Therapy ... 93
Blackberry and Radish Embrace ... 94
Pear goes Pumpkin ... 94
Avocado Avenue ... 95
Broccoli in Nectarine ... 95
Fennel in Chia ... 96
Spinach joins Cashew ... 96

Classic Smoothies

Mint Medley ... 97
Lettuce Nectar ... 97
Watercress and Orange is lovely ... 98
Bok Choy needs Red Grape ... 98
Guava Revelation ... 99
Avocado Mirage ... 99
Broccoli and Apricot Snog ... 100
Fennel and Pineapple Waistline ... 100
Fennel Fantasy ... 101
Green Cabbage loves Kiwi ... 101
Rocket embraces Blackberry ... 102
Mint loves Apricot ... 102
Bok Choy in Nectarine ... 103
Red Cabbage and Cranberry Booster ... 103
Strawberry and Peach Extracted ... 104
Spinach Sensation ... 104
Green Cabbage and Melon Machine ... 105
Watercress in Plum ... 105
Red Cabbage and Peeled Fig Concerto ... 106
Lettuce and Prune Reaction ... 106
Mango Tango ... 107
Cherry Berry ... 107
Red Cabbage meets Melon ... 108
Spinach and Papaya Concerto ... 108
Mint goes Clementine ... 109
Date Kiss ... 109

Carrot Tonic 110
Beetroot Blossom 110
Celeriac Constellation 111
Rocket Rush 111
Spinach Splendour 112
Papaya Royale 112
Lettuce and Pineapple Infusion 113
Plum Job 113
Green Pepper Power 114
Orange Morning 114
Spinach loves Cherry 115
Tangerine needs Tomato 115
Fennel Fix 116
Broccoli and Mint Seduction 116
Banana joins Celery 117
Peeled Fig and Zucchini Sunshine 117
Lettuce and Watercress Waistline 118
Prune and Swede Embrace 118
Bok Choy Elixir 119
Yellow Pepper Cocktail 119
Cranberry and Turnip Treat 120
Green Cabbage Scene 120
Rocket in Clementine 121
Spinach and Pear Perfection 121

Notes 122

The Health Benefits of NutriBullet
Raw Vegetable Variation

Many clinical studies have shown that raw vegetables help fight the big killers today. They help significantly to fight Cancer (the more veggies and the less meat you eat the better your body can prevent and fight tumours). There was a wonderful study done on the Norwegians during the second world war when the German occupiers commandeered all their meat. The result was that the incidence of all types of cancer in Norwegians fell by more than 50%.

They help fight Cardio Vascular Disease. They provide essential antioxidants, oils, minerals, vitamins and are generally better for us than a hamburger or a pork sausage. But the trouble is that they normally do not taste as good as a hamburger or a pork sausage unless they are roasted with cheese or boiled to the point where they have lost most of their goodness.

This is where the NutriBullet comes in. It makes veggies taste great. A nutriblast can taste as good and as invigorating as a steak with fries or a cappuccino with a croissant or a chocolate torte with cream. Your mother would never have had to tell you to: "Eat your Greens" had your family possessed a NutriBullet.

The manufacturers claim all sorts of health benefits from it. And without going into medical detail, whatever the goodness is in a vegetable or leafy green or fruit or nut or seed, the NutriBullet can get that goodness out without destroying the delicate biochemical compounds with heat from cooking them. It is billed not as a blender or a juicer, but as an extractor. This is because the machine represents the best method mankind presently has of extracting the goodness from non meat food. The blades break down the cell walls of the ingredients and thereby release the cell contents into your intestines. So unless you have teeth which can rotate at 10,000 rpm, the NutriBullet represents a significant advance on chewing.

The other psychological trait of mankind which works against us here, is that we are loyal to what we like. Most of retail commerce is based upon brand loyalty. Although this type of loyalty doesn't always work so well with romantic partners! So we find a vegetable we like and then just eat that all the time. I mean once I have a record that I like, I will listen to it over and over again. So even if we do eat some vegetables or leafy greens or fruits, they will tend to be repetitions of a very small selection of what is available. They will just the ones that we have become familiar with and grown to like. They are essentially the vegetable next door.

So the purpose of this book is to empower to reader to vary their vegetables and fruits and greens and nuts and seeds on a daily basis. That is why we have included so many delicious Blasts and Smoothies. If you only drink a small fraction of these NutriBullet recipes you will be deficient in nothing that nature provides from Vegetables, Fruits, Nuts, Seeds and Greens.

Certain amino acids (protein) and fatty acids (fat) vitamins and minerals cannot be manufactured by the body. So they have to be eaten. This is one of the reasons why food variation is so important. Failing to eat certain essential foods can be lethal – even if you are putting on weight from all the food that you are eating! This was discovered when canned liquid diets were first invented. Some of the people who tried these out for more than a month just dropped dead due to running out of essential amino acids.

AMINO ACIDS

Essential Amino Acids

There are 11 of them: Tryptophan, Tyrosine, Threonine, Isoleucine, Histidine Leucine, Lysine, Methionine, Phenylaneline, Cysteine and Valine. These are nicely distributed throughout the leafy greens and although meat and dairy have more protein and therefore more essential amino acids than greens per gram they have less protein than green per kcal. So for dieters, Spinach (yummy) and Kale (if you can stand it) are a good option.

One 200 ml glass of whole milk has between 22-38% of the Recommended Daily Intake of all of the 11 essential amino acids (except Cysteine – 14% of the RDI). We use 200 ml of whole milk in some of our Blast and Smoothie Recipes.

Essential Vitamins

These are: A, B1 (Thiamin), B2 (Riboflavin), B3 (Niacin), B4 (Choline/Adenine)) B5 (Pantotheic Acid), B6 (Pyridoxines), B7 (Biotin)B9 (Folates), B12 (Cobalamin), C, D3, E, K.

Stop Press: The latest EU guidelines for Vitamin D3 are now 4000 IU per day rather than 400! Also the latest research shows that high dose Vitamin D3 toxicity is caused by a lack of Vitamin K2. Spinach and Kale are rich in K1 which the body can convert into K2. But 100 micrograms of K2 supplementation (MK7 variety) is recommended for each 1000 IU of Vitamin D3. Vitamin K2 is expensive so eat your dark leafy greens!

Essential Oils and Fats

This is a very short list. Basically the more fish based Omega3 (EPA DHA in particular) the better up to around 5 grams per day. And the more seed nut or vegetable based Omega3 (ALA) the better without limit.

There is plenty of evidence that Omega 3 in your diet has a large effect upon the cardio vascular system. In particular the Omega3 fish based or vegetable and seed based fatty acids should be eaten in larger amounts if you are on a high fat diet. There are good Omega3 supplements out there but whole foods containing Omega3 normally provide better absorption into the body than Omega3 supplements.

The 10 Essential Minerals

Calcium, Copper, Iron, Magnesium, Manganese, Phosphours, Potassium, Selenium, Sodium, Zinc

SUPERFOODS

25 Widely Recognized Superfoods

These Superfoods contain many of the essential amino acids, fats, vitamins and minerals. But that is not why they are superfoods. They are defined as superfoods due to the health benefits that they confer. They are generally rich in anthocyanins, polyphenols, flavenoids, antioxidants, cancer fighting ellagic acid, heart disease fighting lycopene and other really useful nutrients which whilst not essential (in the sense that they can be manufactured by the body if it has the right components to hand), promote good health, fitness and well being. Between them these Superfoods are attributed with the following health benefits…

Increased Protection from Bacterial and Viral Infections
Increased Immune Function
Reduced Cancer Risk
Protection Against Heart Disease
Slowing Aging
DNA Repair and Protection
Prevention and reduction of Cardiovascular Disease
Reduced Hypertension (High Blood Pressure)
Alzheimer's Protection
Osteoporosis Protection
Stroke Prevention
Reduced Risk of Colon Cancer
Protection Against Heart Disease
Antioxidant Protection
Prevention of Epileptic Seizures
Prevention of Alopecia (Spot Baldness)
Reduced Risk of Type II Diabetes
Reduced Frequency of Migraine Headaches
Alleviation of Premenstrual Syndrome (PMS)
Regulation of Blood Sugar and Insulin Dependence
Slowing the progression of AIDS
Protection Against Dementia
Improved Eye Health

Alleviation of Inflammation
Alleviation of the Common Cold
Improving Sleep depth and length
Detoxing and Cleasning the body
Improving Bones Teeth Nerves and Muscle

Buckwheat and **Quinoa**: Too high in carbs to be included in our list and not suitable for a Blender Recipe

Chili Peppers and Garlic: Great but not really suitable for a Blender Recipe

Almonds: High in Protein, unsaturated Fat, Vitamins B1, B2, B3, B9, E, Calcium, Copper, Iron, Magnesium Phosphorus, Potassium, Zinc and Fibre

Dark Cholcolate: High in Protein, Saturated Fat, Vitamins B1, B2, B3, B9, K, Calcium, Copper, Magnesium Manganese, Phosphorus, Potassium, Selenium, Zinc and Fibre

Flax Seeds: High in Protein, unsaturated Fat, Vitamins B1, B3, B5, B6, B9, Calcium, Copper, Iron, Magnesium, Manganese, Phosphorus, Potassium, Selenium, Zinc, Fibre

Pumpkin Seeds: High in Protein, unsaturated Fat, Vitamins B2, B3, B5, B6, B9, E, Calcium, Copper, Iron, Magnesium, Manganese, Phosphorus, Potassium, Selenium, Zinc

Chia Seeds: High in Protein, has all essential amino acids in good quantity, incredibly high in Fibre at 34%, High in Omega3 at 17%, Vitamins B1, B2, B3, B9, Calcium, Copper Manganese, Phosphorus, Selenium, Zinc

Apricots: High in Vitamins A.C, E, Iron, Potassium, Fibre

Avocados: High in unsaturated Fat, Vitamins B2, B3, B5, B6, B9, C, K Cooper, Magnesium, Manganese and Potassium, Fibre

Blueberries: High in Vitamins B9, C, K, Manganese and Fibre

Raspberries: High in Vitamins B1, B2, B3, B9, C, K, Copper, Iron, Manganese and Fibre

Blackberries: High in Vitamins B9, C, K, Manganese and Fibre

Guavas: High in Vitamins: A, B9, C, Copper, Magnesium, Manganese, Potassium, Fibre

Papaya: High in Vitamins A, B9, C, Potassium, Fiber

Goji Berries: Contains all 11 Essential amino Acids - High in Vitamins A B2 C, Calcium, Selenium, Zinc, Iron, Potassium. But 46% Sugars. So not too many of them. Cures everything from impotence to malaria according to internet hype. Waitrose do them in the UK. Also called Wolfberries

Ginger: High in Vitamins B1, B2, B5, B6, C, Calcium, Copper, Iron, Magnesium, Manganese, Potassium, Selenium, Zinc, Fibre

Broccoli: High in Vitamins A, B1, B2, B5, B6, B9, C, K, Calcium, Iron, Magnesium, Manganese, Potassium

Carrots: High in Vitamins A, B3, B6, B9, C, K, Manganese, Potassium, Fibre

Tomatoes: High in Vitamins A, B2, B6, B9 C, Potassium, Lycopene

Beetroot: Vitamin B6, B9, C, Iron, Magnesium, Manganese, Phosphorus, Potassium, Zinc, Fibre

Kale: High in Vitamins A, B1, B2, B3, B6, B9, C, K, Calcium, Copper, Iron, Magnesium, Manganese, Potassium

Spinach: High in Vitamins A, B2, B6, B9, C, E, K, Calcium, Copper, Iron. Magnesium, Manganese, Potassium, Fibre

Swiss Chard: High in Vitamins A, C, E, K, Calcium, Copper, Iron, Magensium, Manganese, Potassium, Sodium

Hence we include many Superfood Blast and Smoothie Recipes!

Sleep and Foods

As an example of what food can do for you - here is how diet can help you sleep – without having to take sleeping tablets. If you suffer from insomnia then you may be deficient in an essential amino acid called Tryptophan.

The key players in putting your body to sleep are Serotonin, Melatonin, 5HTP and Tryptophan. All of these can be purchased from health food shops.

The chemical pathway works like this. First the body converts Tryptophan into Tryptophan Hydroxylase (or 5 HydroxyTryptophan or 5HTP). Then this, together with Vitamins. B3, B6, B9 and Magnesium is used to synthesize the neurotransmitter Serotonin. The Serotonin is then converted to the neurohormone Melatonin as necessary

Serotonin is the body's natural sedative. The higher your serotonin levels are the more sleepy you feel. Melatonin controls your body clock, your circadian rhythm, your sleep cycle. These two hormones both put you to sleep and determine how long and how good your sleep quality is.

Tryptophan is one of the essential amino acids – which means that it is essential for human life and the body cannot manufacture it. So we have to eat it!

Just taking 1 gram of Tryptophan can significantly decrease the time it takes to fall asleep and the time you stay asleep for. 6 grams are used to treat certain forms of PMS. 3 grams per day for 2 weeks is prescribed to treat depression and anxiety without the side effects associated with clinical anti depressants like Prosac.So to cheer yourself up eat some foods which are rich in Tryptophan!

Foods which are high in Tryptophan include Chocolate, Eggs, Cheese, Brown rice, Avocados, Walnuts, Peanuts, Meats, Sesame seeds, Sunflower seeds and Pumpkin seeds. So having a cup of cocoa before you go to bed has a sound basis in biochemistry!

Best Seeds	Tryptophan /100g	Best Greens	Tryptophan /100g
Chia Seeds	721 mg	Parsely	45 mg
Pumpkin Seeds	576 mg	Spinach	39 mg
Sesame Seeds	388 mg	Kale	34 mg
Sunflower Seeds	348 mg	Broccoli	33 mg
Flax Seed	297 mg	Watercress	30 mg
		Swiss Chard	17 mg
		Bok Choy	15 mg

Best Nuts	Tryptophan /100g	Best Veggies	Tryptophan /100g
Cashew Nuts	470 mg	Cauliflower	20 mg
Peanuts	340 mg	Beetroot	19 mg
Walnuts	318 mg	Fine Beans	19 mg
Pistachio Nuts	284 mg	Carrot	12 mg
Almonds	214 mg	Zucchini	10 mg
Hazelnuts	193 mg		
Brazil Nuts	141 mg		
Pecans	93 mg		

Best Fruits	Tryptophan /100g	Foods	Tryptophan /100g
Avocado	26 mg	Cocoa Powder	283 mg
Prunes	25 mg	Dairy Milk	40 mg
Apricots	12 mg	Cheddar Cheese	515 mg
Dates	12 mg	Mozarella Cheese	558 mg
Grapes	11 mg	Egg	210 mg
Oranges	10 mg		
Peaches	10 mg		
Plums	9 mg		
Grapefruits	9 mg		

Some of our NutriBullet Recipes are designed to deliver Tryptophan. The RDI is 285 mg. But for a good nights sleep 1000 mg is better. Lots of Chia seeds Cashews Milk Spinach and Prunes and some Cocoa powder will get you to around 475 mg of Tryptophan from one NutriBlast. That is 166% of the RDI. But you would need 2 of them to really help with sleep that night. Alternatively eat 100 gram of cheese, that would give you another 500 mg of Tryptophan.

Game meat poultry and eggs are also great non nutribullet sources of Tryptophan. If you need something stronger then consider taking the intermediary between Tryptophan and Serotonin - 5HTP as a supplement. Double-blind studies have shown that 5HTP is as effective as Prozac, Paxil, Zoloft, Imipramine and Desipramine and it has less side effects being a natural body compound. 5HTP is cheaper and non prescription being a regular dietary supplement.

Eat a Rainbow of Colour

Red – Lyopene, anthocyanins and other phytonutrients found in red fruits and veggies. Lycopene is a powerful antioxidant that can help reduce the risk of cancer and keep our heart healthy and improve memory function.

White/Tan – Contrary to popular belief, white foods aren't so useless after all! These foods have been shown to reduce the risk of certain cancers, balance hormone levels, lower blood pressure, and boost your body's natural immunity with nutrients such as EGCG and allicin. White fruits and vegetables contain a range of health-promoting phytochemicals such as allicin (found in garlic) which is known for its antiviral and antibacterial properties. Some members of the white group, such as bananas and potatoes, are also a good source of potassium.

Green – Chlorophyll-rich detoxification properties are the most noted value in leafy greens. In addition, luteins, zeaxanthin, along with indoles, help boost greens' cancer-fighting properties, encourage vision health, and help build strong bones and teeth. Green vegetables contain a range of phytochemicals including carotenoids, indoles and saponins, all of which have anti-cancer properties. Leafy greens such as spinach and broccoli are also excellent sources of folate.

Blue/Purple – Phytochemicals anthocyanin and resveratrol promote youthful skin, hair and nails. In addition, these anti-inflammatory compounds may also play a role in cancer-prevention, especially skin cancer and urinary and digestive tract health. They may also reduce the risk of cardio vascular disease.

Orange/Yellow – Foods glowing with orange and yellow are great immune-boosters and vision protectors, mainly due to their high levels of carotenoids. Carotenoids give this group their vibrant colour. A well-known carotenoid called Betacarotene is found in sweet potatoes, pumpkins and carrots. It is converted to vitamin A, which helps maintain healthy mucous membranes and healthy eyes. Another carotenoid called lutein is stored in the eye and has been found to prevent cataracts and age-related macular degeneration, which can lead to blindness.

Nutrition Data

All our Blasts and Smoothies come with full nutritional data giving the precise number of grams of Protein, Carbohydrate, Fat and Fibre for each recipe and the number of Kcals it contains. The data is taken mainly from the USDA database.

NutriBullet Capacities

US traditional cup is 8 US fluid oz or 240 ml (236 ml to be exact). However putting berries or slices or cubes of fruit and veggies into a cup wastes around 50% of the space so in weight terms an 8 fluid oz cup will contain around 4 oz or 120 grams of contents.

Greens use even less of the space, so 1 Cups/Handfuls of Spinach or Kale will only weigh around 40 grams or 1½ oz – even after pressing it down a bit.

There are 28.35 grams in a British Imperial fluid ounce, which is 4% larger than the US fluid ounce - which is pretty unhelpful. So it is easier just to take 28 grams for an ounce in both cases.

The NutriBullet tall cup takes 590 ml/grams of water up to the MAX fill line. The small cup takes 305 grams of water up to the MAX fill line. *All our recipes are designed and stated for the standard tall cup* (28 oz total, 24 oz to max fill).

To use the small cup you just halve them all!

The entire tall cup can take around 826 ml/grams of water up to the top. This is 3½ standard US cups or 28 fluid ounces. However we can put 4¼ cups worth of greens, veggies, fruits, nuts and seeds into the tall cup because they compress a lot when they lose their shape after blasting.

All ingredients are stated in Cups and Handfuls or Grams and American Ounces (oz)

Warnings

Do not put your hand or any implement near the blades when the NutriBullet is plugged in to an electricity supply.

Cleaning

The NutriBullet is easy to clean. The manufacturers recommend warm water (not hot) and a mild detergent. Rinse the blades and the cups and the base (if necessary) immediately after use to prevent the debris from drying.

Authors Preference for Kale

Kale is a Superfood and is very good for you. But it does not taste as good as the other greens in a NutriBlast in our opinion! To be frank, it tastes like cardboard. So we have excluded it from these recipes. It is better to fry it in some olive oil.

AVOID THESE INGREDIENTS: Apple Pear Peach Plum Apricot and Cherry **stones and pips** contain cyanide which is very poisonous. These stones and pips *must* therefore be removed before use!

Rhubarb leaves contain oxalate which causes kidney stones, comas, convulsions. 5lb of Rhubarb leaves is fatal!

Tomatoes are fine but the **tomato leaves and vines** are not. They contain alkaloid poisons such as atropine which causes headaches dizziness and vomiting.

Nutmeg: Contains myristicine which is halucingoenic and causes dizziness and vomiting. It is OK in small quantities as a spice but we do not recommend it for the NutriBullet.

Kidney Beans and **Lima Beans**: These are really really poisonous if eaten raw.

Tips and Extras

Cinnamon and Cloves are lovely in a hot drink but do not really work in a cold one such as a Nutribullet blast. We cannot recommend adding sugar given the health difficulties associated with refined sucrose. But the following are fantastic in Nutriblasts…

Ginger Root (sliced)
Lemon Juice
Lime Juice
Agave Nectar
Honey
Garlic Cloves
Cocoa Powder which is also called Cacao Powder (a Superfood)
85% Dark Chocolate (a Superfood)
Maca Powder (a Superfood)
Instant Coffee
Coriander
Parsley
Sage
Chives
Chlorella Powder (Detoxing supergreen nutrient rich algae)
Spirulina Powder (Protein and nutrient rich supergreen immunity boosting algae)
Whey Protein Powder (Banana, Chocolate, Cookies, Strawberry flavours etc.) - for extra protein
Rice Protein Powder
Pea Protein Powder
Soy Protein Powder

These can be added to any of the recipes for a taste or nutrition boost.

THE RECIPES

Superfood Smoothies
Made entirely out of Superfoods

Chard on Apricot

Ingredients

1 Cup/Handful of Black Kale de-stemmed (40 grams or 1½ oz)
1 Cup/Handful of Swiss Chard (40 grams or 1½ oz)
1 Cup/Handful of Papaya (120 grams or 4 oz)
1 Cup/Handful of Apricot halves (120 grams or 4 oz)
150 ml / 5 fl oz of Almond Milk (Unsweetened)

Protein 5g, Fat 3g, Carb 24g, Fibre 7g, 150 Kcals

Preparation

Put all the solid ingredients into the Tall Cup and press them down below the Max Line. Add the fluid base to fill the cup up to the Max Line. Screw the Nutribullet Extractor Blade on to the top of the cup. Invert the cup, press it down into the Nutribullet Power Base and twist it into place. Blast the mixture until it is really smooth (20 or so seconds). **Enjoy!**

Broccoli Blockbuster

Ingredients

1 Cup/Handful of Spinach (40 grams or 1½ oz)
1 Cup/Handful of Broccoli Florets (40 grams or 1½ oz)
1 Cup/Handful of Blueberries (120 grams or 4 oz)
½ Cup of Goji Berries Dried (40 grams or 1½ oz)
150 ml / 5 fl oz of Dairy Milk Whole

Protein 14g, Fat 7g, Carb 47g, Fibre 7g, 315 Kcals

Preparation

Put all the solid ingredients into the Tall Cup and press them down below the Max Line. Add the fluid base to fill the cup up to the Max Line. Screw the Nutribullet Extractor Blade on to the top of the cup. Invert the cup, press it down into the Nutribullet Power Base and twist it into place. Blast the mixture until it is really smooth (20 or so seconds). **Enjoy!**

Blackberry and Raspberry Piazza

Ingredients

1 Cup/Handful of Spinach (40 grams or 1½ oz)
1 Cup/Handful of Swiss Chard (40 grams or 1½ oz)
1 Cup/Handful of Blackberries (120 grams or 4 oz)
1 Cup/Handful of Raspberries (120 grams or 4 oz)
150 ml / 5 fl oz of Dairy Milk Whole

Protein 10g, Fat 7g, Carb 20g, Fibre 16g, 226 Kcals

Preparation

Put all the solid ingredients into the Tall Cup and press them down below the Max Line. Add the fluid base to fill the cup up to the Max Line. Screw the Nutribullet Extractor Blade on to the top of the cup. Invert the cup, press it down into the Nutribullet Power Base and twist it into place. Blast the mixture until it is really smooth (20 or so seconds). **Enjoy!**

Broccoli and Avocado Fiesta

Ingredients

1 Cup/Handful of Black Kale de-stemmed (40 grams or 1½ oz)
1 Cup/Handful of Broccoli Florets (40 grams or 1½ oz)
1 Cup/Handful of Guava (120 grams or 4 oz)
1 Cup/Handful of Avocado slices (120 grams or 4 oz)
150 ml / 5 fl oz of Almond Milk (Unsweetened)

Protein 9g, Fat 21g, Carb 15g, Fibre 17g, 320 Kcals

Preparation

Put all the solid ingredients into the Tall Cup and press them down below the Max Line. Add the fluid base to fill the cup up to the Max Line. Screw the Nutribullet Extractor Blade on to the top of the cup. Invert the cup, press it down into the Nutribullet Power Base and twist it into place. Blast the mixture until it is really smooth (20 or so seconds). **Enjoy!**

Spinach and Guava Boost

Ingredients

1 Cup/Handful of Swiss Chard (40 grams or 1½ oz)
1 Cup/Handful of Spinach (40 grams or 1½ oz)
1 Cup/Handful of Guava (120 grams or 4 oz)
½ Cup of Goji Berries Dried (40 grams or 1½ oz)
150 ml / 5 fl oz of Almond Milk (Unsweetened)

Protein 11g, Fat 4g, Carb 35g, Fibre 11g, 246 Kcals

Preparation

Put all the solid ingredients into the Tall Cup and press them down below the Max Line. Add the fluid base to fill the cup up to the Max Line. Screw the Nutribullet Extractor Blade on to the top of the cup. Invert the cup, press it down into the Nutribullet Power Base and twist it into place. Blast the mixture until it is really smooth (20 or so seconds). **Enjoy!**

Apricot needs Raspberry

Ingredients

1 Cup/Handful of Black Kale de-stemmed (40 grams or 1½ oz)
1 Cup/Handful of Broccoli Florets (40 grams or 1½ oz)
1 Cup/Handful of Apricot halves (120 grams or 4 oz)
1 Cup/Handful of Raspberries (120 grams or 4 oz)
150 ml / 5 fl oz of Dairy Milk Whole

Protein 10g, Fat 7g, Carb 27g, Fibre 12g, 243 Kcals

Preparation

Put all the solid ingredients into the Tall Cup and press them down below the Max Line. Add the fluid base to fill the cup up to the Max Line. Screw the Nutribullet Extractor Blade on to the top of the cup. Invert the cup, press it down into the Nutribullet Power Base and twist it into place. Blast the mixture until it is really smooth (20 or so seconds). **Enjoy!**

Broccoli goes Papaya

Ingredients

1 Cup/Handful of Black Kale de-stemmed (40 grams or 1½ oz)
1 Cup/Handful of Broccoli Florets (40 grams or 1½ oz)
1 Cup/Handful of Blackberries (120 grams or 4 oz)
1 Cup/Handful of Papaya (120 grams or 4 oz)
150 ml / 5 fl oz of Almond Milk (Unsweetened)

Protein 5g, Fat 3g, Carb 19g, Fibre 11g, 150 Kcals

Preparation

Put all the solid ingredients into the Tall Cup and press them down below the Max Line. Add the fluid base to fill the cup up to the Max Line. Screw the Nutribullet Extractor Blade on to the top of the cup. Invert the cup, press it down into the Nutribullet Power Base and twist it into place. Blast the mixture until it is really smooth (20 or so seconds). **Enjoy!**

Blueberry Boost

Ingredients

1 Cup/Handful of Spinach (40 grams or 1½ oz)
1 Cup/Handful of Swiss Chard (40 grams or 1½ oz)
1 Cup/Handful of Blueberries (120 grams or 4 oz)
1 Cup/Handful of Avocado slices (120 grams or 4 oz)
150 ml / 5 fl oz of Dairy Milk Whole

Protein 10g, Fat 24g, Carb 25g, Fibre 12g, 373 Kcals

Preparation

Put all the solid ingredients into the Tall Cup and press them down below the Max Line. Add the fluid base to fill the cup up to the Max Line. Screw the Nutribullet Extractor Blade on to the top of the cup. Invert the cup, press it down into the Nutribullet Power Base and twist it into place. Blast the mixture until it is really smooth (20 or so seconds). **Enjoy!**

Chard joins Raspberry

Ingredients

1 Cup/Handful of Broccoli Florets (40 grams or 1½ oz)
1 Cup/Handful of Swiss Chard (40 grams or 1½ oz)
1 Cup/Handful of Guava (120 grams or 4 oz)
1 Cup/Handful of Raspberries (120 grams or 4 oz)
150 ml / 5 fl oz of Almond Milk (Unsweetened)

Protein 7g, Fat 4g, Carb 20g, Fibre 17g, 184 Kcals

Preparation

Put all the solid ingredients into the Tall Cup and press them down below the Max Line. Add the fluid base to fill the cup up to the Max Line. Screw the Nutribullet Extractor Blade on to the top of the cup. Invert the cup, press it down into the Nutribullet Power Base and twist it into place. Blast the mixture until it is really smooth (20 or so seconds). **Enjoy!**

Spinach embraces Papaya

Ingredients

1 Cup/Handful of Spinach (40 grams or 1½ oz)
1 Cup/Handful of Black Kale de-stemmed (40 grams or 1½ oz)
1 Cup/Handful of Papaya (120 grams or 4 oz)
½ Cup of Goji Berries Dried (40 grams or 1½ oz)
150 ml / 5 fl oz of Dairy Milk Whole

Protein 14g, Fat 7g, Carb 42g, Fibre 6g, 299 Kcals

Preparation

Put all the solid ingredients into the Tall Cup and press them down below the Max Line. Add the fluid base to fill the cup up to the Max Line. Screw the Nutribullet Extractor Blade on to the top of the cup. Invert the cup, press it down into the Nutribullet Power Base and twist it into place. Blast the mixture until it is really smooth (20 or so seconds). **Enjoy!**

Chard and Blueberry Revision

Ingredients

1 Cup/Handful of Black Kale de-stemmed (40 grams or 1½ oz)
1 Cup/Handful of Swiss Chard (40 grams or 1½ oz)
1 Cup/Handful of Blueberries (120 grams or 4 oz)
1 Cup/Handful of Blackberries (120 grams or 4 oz)
150 ml / 5 fl oz of Almond Milk (Unsweetened)

Protein 5g, Fat 3g, Carb 21g, Fibre 11g, 161 Kcals

Preparation

Put all the solid ingredients into the Tall Cup and press them down below the Max Line. Add the fluid base to fill the cup up to the Max Line. Screw the Nutribullet Extractor Blade on to the top of the cup. Invert the cup, press it down into the Nutribullet Power Base and twist it into place. Blast the mixture until it is really smooth (20 or so seconds). **Enjoy!**

Spinach and Apricot Therapy

Ingredients

1 Cup/Handful of Broccoli Florets (40 grams or 1½ oz)
1 Cup/Handful of Spinach (40 grams or 1½ oz)
1 Cup/Handful of Avocado slices (120 grams or 4 oz)
1 Cup/Handful of Apricot halves (120 grams or 4 oz)
150 ml / 5 fl oz of Dairy Milk Whole

Protein 11g, Fat 24g, Carb 22g, Fibre 12g, 368 Kcals

Preparation

Put all the solid ingredients into the Tall Cup and press them down below the Max Line. Add the fluid base to fill the cup up to the Max Line. Screw the Nutribullet Extractor Blade on to the top of the cup. Invert the cup, press it down into the Nutribullet Power Base and twist it into place. Blast the mixture until it is really smooth (20 or so seconds). **Enjoy!**

Chard Crush

Ingredients

1 Cup/Handful of Broccoli Florets (40 grams or 1½ oz)
1 Cup/Handful of Swiss Chard (40 grams or 1½ oz)
1 Cup/Handful of Apricot halves (120 grams or 4 oz)
1 Cup/Handful of Guava (120 grams or 4 oz)
150 ml / 5 fl oz of Almond Milk (Unsweetened)

Protein 7g, Fat 3g, Carb 24g, Fibre 11g, 179 Kcals

Preparation

Put all the solid ingredients into the Tall Cup and press them down below the Max Line. Add the fluid base to fill the cup up to the Max Line. Screw the Nutribullet Extractor Blade on to the top of the cup. Invert the cup, press it down into the Nutribullet Power Base and twist it into place. Blast the mixture until it is really smooth (20 or so seconds). **Enjoy!**

Black Kale in Avocado

Ingredients

1 Cup/Handful of Spinach (40 grams or 1½ oz)
1 Cup/Handful of Black Kale de-stemmed (40 grams or 1½ oz)
1 Cup/Handful of Avocado slices (120 grams or 4 oz)
1 Cup/Handful of Papaya (120 grams or 4 oz)
150 ml / 5 fl oz of Dairy Milk Whole

Protein 10g, Fat 24g, Carb 21g, Fibre 12g, 362 Kcals

Preparation

Put all the solid ingredients into the Tall Cup and press them down below the Max Line. Add the fluid base to fill the cup up to the Max Line. Screw the Nutribullet Extractor Blade on to the top of the cup. Invert the cup, press it down into the Nutribullet Power Base and twist it into place. Blast the mixture until it is really smooth (20 or so seconds). **Enjoy!**

Black Kale Bonanza

Ingredients

1 Cup/Handful of Spinach (40 grams or 1½ oz)
1 Cup/Handful of Black Kale de-stemmed (40 grams or 1½ oz)
½ Cup of Goji Berries Dried (40 grams or 1½ oz)
1 Cup/Handful of Blueberries (120 grams or 4 oz)
150 ml / 5 fl oz of Almond Milk (Unsweetened)

Protein 10g, Fat 4g, Carb 39g, Fibre 7g, 239 Kcals

Preparation

Put all the solid ingredients into the Tall Cup and press them down below the Max Line. Add the fluid base to fill the cup up to the Max Line. Screw the Nutribullet Extractor Blade on to the top of the cup. Invert the cup, press it down into the Nutribullet Power Base and twist it into place. Blast the mixture until it is really smooth (20 or so seconds). **Enjoy!**

Broccoli meets Blackberry

Ingredients

1 Cup/Handful of Swiss Chard (40 grams or 1½ oz)
1 Cup/Handful of Broccoli Florets (40 grams or 1½ oz)
1 Cup/Handful of Raspberries (120 grams or 4 oz)
1 Cup/Handful of Blackberries (120 grams or 4 oz)
150 ml / 5 fl oz of Dairy Milk Whole

Protein 10g, Fat 7g, Carb 21g, Fibre 16g, 231 Kcals

Preparation

Put all the solid ingredients into the Tall Cup and press them down below the Max Line. Add the fluid base to fill the cup up to the Max Line. Screw the Nutribullet Extractor Blade on to the top of the cup. Invert the cup, press it down into the Nutribullet Power Base and twist it into place. Blast the mixture until it is really smooth (20 or so seconds). **Enjoy!**

Chard loves Guava

Ingredients

1 Cup/Handful of Black Kale de-stemmed (40 grams or 1½ oz)
1 Cup/Handful of Swiss Chard (40 grams or 1½ oz)
1 Cup/Handful of Guava (120 grams or 4 oz)
1 Cup/Handful of Papaya (120 grams or 4 oz)
150 ml / 5 fl oz of Dairy Milk Whole

Protein 11g, Fat 8g, Carb 30g, Fibre 10g, 250 Kcals

Preparation

Put all the solid ingredients into the Tall Cup and press them down below the Max Line. Add the fluid base to fill the cup up to the Max Line. Screw the Nutribullet Extractor Blade on to the top of the cup. Invert the cup, press it down into the Nutribullet Power Base and twist it into place. Blast the mixture until it is really smooth (20 or so seconds). **Enjoy!**

Spinach Sunset

Ingredients

1 Cup/Handful of Broccoli Florets (40 grams or 1½ oz)
1 Cup/Handful of Spinach (40 grams or 1½ oz)
1 Cup/Handful of Apricot halves (120 grams or 4 oz)
½ Cup of Goji Berries Dried (40 grams or 1½ oz)
150 ml / 5 fl oz of Almond Milk (Unsweetened)

Protein 10g, Fat 3g, Carb 36g, Fibre 7g, 228 Kcals

Preparation

Put all the solid ingredients into the Tall Cup and press them down below the Max Line. Add the fluid base to fill the cup up to the Max Line. Screw the Nutribullet Extractor Blade on to the top of the cup. Invert the cup, press it down into the Nutribullet Power Base and twist it into place. Blast the mixture until it is really smooth (20 or so seconds). **Enjoy!**

Spinach and Blueberry Concerto

Ingredients

1 Cup/Handful of Spinach (40 grams or 1½ oz)
1 Cup/Handful of Broccoli Florets (40 grams or 1½ oz)
1 Cup/Handful of Avocado slices (120 grams or 4 oz)
1 Cup/Handful of Blueberries (120 grams or 4 oz)
150 ml / 5 fl oz of Almond Milk (Unsweetened)

Protein 6g, Fat 20g, Carb 19g, Fibre 13g, 302 Kcals

Preparation

Put all the solid ingredients into the Tall Cup and press them down below the Max Line. Add the fluid base to fill the cup up to the Max Line. Screw the Nutribullet Extractor Blade on to the top of the cup. Invert the cup, press it down into the Nutribullet Power Base and twist it into place. Blast the mixture until it is really smooth (20 or so seconds). **Enjoy!**

Black Kale in Blackberry

Ingredients

1 Cup/Handful of Black Kale de-stemmed (40 grams or 1½ oz)
1 Cup/Handful of Swiss Chard (40 grams or 1½ oz)
1 Cup/Handful of Blackberries (120 grams or 4 oz)
1 Cup/Handful of Raspberries (120 grams or 4 oz)
150 ml / 5 fl oz of Dairy Milk Whole

Protein 10g, Fat 7g, Carb 20g, Fibre 16g, 231 Kcals

Preparation

Put all the solid ingredients into the Tall Cup and press them down below the Max Line. Add the fluid base to fill the cup up to the Max Line. Screw the Nutribullet Extractor Blade on to the top of the cup. Invert the cup, press it down into the Nutribullet Power Base and twist it into place. Blast the mixture until it is really smooth (20 or so seconds). **Enjoy!**

Superfood Blasts
Made entirely out of Superfoods

Black Kale goes Blueberry

Ingredients

1 Cup/Handful of Swiss Chard (40 grams or 1½ oz)
1 Cup/Handful of Black Kale de-stemmed (40 grams or 1½ oz)
½ Cup of Goji Berries Dried (40 grams or 1½ oz)
1 Cup/Handful of Blueberries (120 grams or 4 oz)
22 grams or ¾ oz of Flax Seeds
150 ml / 5 fl oz of Almond Milk (Unsweetened)

Protein 13g, Fat 13g, Carb 39g, Fibre 13g, 355 Kcals

Preparation

Place the nuts or seeds into the Tall Cup. Screw the Nutribullet Extractor Blade on to the top of the cup. Invert the cup, press it down into the Nutribullet Power Base and twist it into place. Blast them for 30 seconds. Put the rest of the solid ingredients into the cup and press them down below the Max Line. Add the fluid base to fill the cup up to the Max Line. Screw the Nutribullet Extractor Blade on to the top of the cup. Invert the cup, press it down into the Nutribullet Power Base and twist it into place. Blast the mixture until it is really smooth (20 or so seconds). **Enjoy!**

Spinach meets Pumpkin

Ingredients

1 Cup/Handful of Broccoli Florets (40 grams or 1½ oz)
1 Cup/Handful of Spinach (40 grams or 1½ oz)
1 Cup/Handful of Avocado slices (120 grams or 4 oz)
1 Cup/Handful of Blackberries (120 grams or 4 oz)
22 grams or ¾ oz of Pumpkin Seeds
150 ml / 5 fl oz of Dairy Milk Whole

Protein 16g, Fat 34g, Carb 19g, Fibre 17g, 486 Kcals

Preparation

Place the nuts or seeds into the Tall Cup. Screw the Nutribullet Extractor Blade on to the top of the cup. Invert the cup, press it down into the Nutribullet Power Base and twist it into place. Blast them for 30 seconds. Put the rest of the solid ingredients into the cup and press them down below the Max Line. Add the fluid base to fill the cup up to the Max Line. Screw the Nutribullet Extractor Blade on to the top of the cup. Invert the cup, press it down into the Nutribullet Power Base and twist it into place. Blast the mixture until it is really smooth (20 or so seconds). **Enjoy!**

Almond Amazement

Ingredients

1 Cup/Handful of Broccoli Florets (40 grams or 1½ oz)
1 Cup/Handful of Spinach (40 grams or 1½ oz)
1 Cup/Handful of Apricot halves (120 grams or 4 oz)
1 Cup/Handful of Papaya (120 grams or 4 oz)
30 grams or 1 oz of Almonds
150 ml / 5 fl oz of Almond Milk (Unsweetened)

Protein 11g, Fat 19g, Carb 26g, Fibre 10g, 328 Kcals

Preparation

Place the nuts or seeds into the Tall Cup. Screw the Nutribullet Extractor Blade on to the top of the cup. Invert the cup, press it down into the Nutribullet Power Base and twist it into place. Blast them for 30 seconds. Put the rest of the solid ingredients into the cup and press them down below the Max Line. Add the fluid base to fill the cup up to the Max Line. Screw the Nutribullet Extractor Blade on to the top of the cup. Invert the cup, press it down into the Nutribullet Power Base and twist it into place. Blast the mixture until it is really smooth (20 or so seconds). **Enjoy!**

Guava loves Chia

Ingredients

1 Cup/Handful of Swiss Chard (40 grams or 1½ oz)
1 Cup/Handful of Black Kale de-stemmed (40 grams or 1½ oz)
1 Cup/Handful of Guava (120 grams or 4 oz)
1 Cup/Handful of Raspberries (120 grams or 4 oz)
22 grams or ¾ oz of Chia Seeds
150 ml / 5 fl oz of Dairy Milk Whole

Protein 15g, Fat 15g, Carb 28g, Fibre 23g, 368 Kcals

Preparation

Place the nuts or seeds into the Tall Cup. Screw the Nutribullet Extractor Blade on to the top of the cup. Invert the cup, press it down into the Nutribullet Power Base and twist it into place. Blast them for 30 seconds. Put the rest of the solid ingredients into the cup and press them down below the Max Line. Add the fluid base to fill the cup up to the Max Line. Screw the Nutribullet Extractor Blade on to the top of the cup. Invert the cup, press it down into the Nutribullet Power Base and twist it into place. Blast the mixture until it is really smooth (20 or so seconds). **Enjoy!**

Blackberry and Flax Elixir

Ingredients

1 Cup/Handful of Broccoli Florets (40 grams or 1½ oz)
1 Cup/Handful of Swiss Chard (40 grams or 1½ oz)
1 Cup/Handful of Blackberries (120 grams or 4 oz)
1 Cup/Handful of Blueberries (120 grams or 4 oz)
22 grams or ¾ oz of Flax Seeds
150 ml / 5 fl oz of Dairy Milk Whole

Protein 13g, Fat 16g, Carb 30g, Fibre 17g, 354 Kcals

Preparation

Place the nuts or seeds into the Tall Cup. Screw the Nutribullet Extractor Blade on to the top of the cup. Invert the cup, press it down into the Nutribullet Power Base and twist it into place. Blast them for 30 seconds. Put the rest of the solid ingredients into the cup and press them down below the Max Line. Add the fluid base to fill the cup up to the Max Line. Screw the Nutribullet Extractor Blade on to the top of the cup. Invert the cup, press it down into the Nutribullet Power Base and twist it into place. Blast the mixture until it is really smooth (20 or so seconds). **Enjoy!**

Raspberry and Pumpkin Consortium

Ingredients

1 Cup/Handful of Spinach (40 grams or 1½ oz)
1 Cup/Handful of Black Kale de-stemmed (40 grams or 1½ oz)
1 Cup/Handful of Raspberries (120 grams or 4 oz)
1 Cup/Handful of Avocado slices (120 grams or 4 oz)
22 grams or ¾ oz of Pumpkin Seeds
150 ml / 5 fl oz of Almond Milk (Unsweetened)

Protein 12g, Fat 30g, Carb 12g, Fibre 19g, 421 Kcals

Preparation

Place the nuts or seeds into the Tall Cup. Screw the Nutribullet Extractor Blade on to the top of the cup. Invert the cup, press it down into the Nutribullet Power Base and twist it into place. Blast them for 30 seconds. Put the rest of the solid ingredients into the cup and press them down below the Max Line. Add the fluid base to fill the cup up to the Max Line. Screw the Nutribullet Extractor Blade on to the top of the cup. Invert the cup, press it down into the Nutribullet Power Base and twist it into place. Blast the mixture until it is really smooth (20 or so seconds). **Enjoy!**

Goji Gala

Ingredients

1 Cup/Handful of Swiss Chard (40 grams or 1½ oz)
1 Cup/Handful of Spinach (40 grams or 1½ oz)
½ Cup of Goji Berries Dried (40 grams or 1½ oz)
1 Cup/Handful of Apricot halves (120 grams or 4 oz)
30 grams or 1 oz of Almonds
150 ml / 5 fl oz of Almond Milk (Unsweetened)

Protein 16g, Fat 19g, Carb 37g, Fibre 10g, 399 Kcals

Preparation

Place the nuts or seeds into the Tall Cup. Screw the Nutribullet Extractor Blade on to the top of the cup. Invert the cup, press it down into the Nutribullet Power Base and twist it into place. Blast them for 30 seconds. Put the rest of the solid ingredients into the cup and press them down below the Max Line. Add the fluid base to fill the cup up to the Max Line. Screw the Nutribullet Extractor Blade on to the top of the cup. Invert the cup, press it down into the Nutribullet Power Base and twist it into place. Blast the mixture until it is really smooth (20 or so seconds). **Enjoy!**

Guava Galaxy

Ingredients

1 Cup/Handful of Black Kale de-stemmed (40 grams or 1½ oz)
1 Cup/Handful of Broccoli Florets (40 grams or 1½ oz)
1 Cup/Handful of Papaya (120 grams or 4 oz)
1 Cup/Handful of Guava (120 grams or 4 oz)
22 grams or ¾ oz of Chia Seeds
150 ml / 5 fl oz of Dairy Milk Whole

Protein 15g, Fat 14g, Carb 33g, Fibre 18g, 363 Kcals

Preparation

Place the nuts or seeds into the Tall Cup. Screw the Nutribullet Extractor Blade on to the top of the cup. Invert the cup, press it down into the Nutribullet Power Base and twist it into place. Blast them for 30 seconds. Put the rest of the solid ingredients into the cup and press them down below the Max Line. Add the fluid base to fill the cup up to the Max Line. Screw the Nutribullet Extractor Blade on to the top of the cup. Invert the cup, press it down into the Nutribullet Power Base and twist it into place. Blast the mixture until it is really smooth (20 or so seconds). **Enjoy!**

Spinach joins Raspberry

Ingredients

1 Cup/Handful of Broccoli Florets (40 grams or 1½ oz)
1 Cup/Handful of Spinach (40 grams or 1½ oz)
1 Cup/Handful of Guava (120 grams or 4 oz)
1 Cup/Handful of Raspberries (120 grams or 4 oz)
22 grams or ¾ oz of Chia Seeds
150 ml / 5 fl oz of Almond Milk (Unsweetened)

Protein 11g, Fat 11g, Carb 21g, Fibre 24g, 293 Kcals

Preparation

Place the nuts or seeds into the Tall Cup. Screw the Nutribullet Extractor Blade on to the top of the cup. Invert the cup, press it down into the Nutribullet Power Base and twist it into place. Blast them for 30 seconds. Put the rest of the solid ingredients into the cup and press them down below the Max Line. Add the fluid base to fill the cup up to the Max Line. Screw the Nutribullet Extractor Blade on to the top of the cup. Invert the cup, press it down into the Nutribullet Power Base and twist it into place. Blast the mixture until it is really smooth (20 or so seconds). **Enjoy!**

Avocado Adventure

Ingredients

1 Cup/Handful of Swiss Chard (40 grams or 1½ oz)
1 Cup/Handful of Black Kale de-stemmed (40 grams or 1½ oz)
1 Cup/Handful of Blackberries (120 grams or 4 oz)
1 Cup/Handful of Avocado slices (120 grams or 4 oz)
22 grams or ¾ oz of Pumpkin Seeds
150 ml / 5 fl oz of Dairy Milk Whole

Protein 16g, Fat 34g, Carb 18g, Fibre 17g, 485 Kcals

Preparation

Place the nuts or seeds into the Tall Cup. Screw the Nutribullet Extractor Blade on to the top of the cup. Invert the cup, press it down into the Nutribullet Power Base and twist it into place. Blast them for 30 seconds. Put the rest of the solid ingredients into the cup and press them down below the Max Line. Add the fluid base to fill the cup up to the Max Line. Screw the Nutribullet Extractor Blade on to the top of the cup. Invert the cup, press it down into the Nutribullet Power Base and twist it into place. Blast the mixture until it is really smooth (20 or so seconds). **Enjoy!**

Broccoli embraces Blueberry

Ingredients

1 Cup/Handful of Swiss Chard (40 grams or 1½ oz)
1 Cup/Handful of Broccoli Florets (40 grams or 1½ oz)
1 Cup/Handful of Apricot halves (120 grams or 4 oz)
1 Cup/Handful of Blueberries (120 grams or 4 oz)
30 grams or 1 oz of Almonds
150 ml / 5 fl oz of Dairy Milk Whole

Protein 16g, Fat 22g, Carb 37g, Fibre 10g, 420 Kcals

Preparation

Place the nuts or seeds into the Tall Cup. Screw the Nutribullet Extractor Blade on to the top of the cup. Invert the cup, press it down into the Nutribullet Power Base and twist it into place. Blast them for 30 seconds. Put the rest of the solid ingredients into the cup and press them down below the Max Line. Add the fluid base to fill the cup up to the Max Line. Screw the Nutribullet Extractor Blade on to the top of the cup. Invert the cup, press it down into the Nutribullet Power Base and twist it into place. Blast the mixture until it is really smooth (20 or so seconds). **Enjoy!**

Flax Fiesta

Ingredients

1 Cup/Handful of Spinach (40 grams or 1½ oz)
1 Cup/Handful of Black Kale de-stemmed (40 grams or 1½ oz)
½ Cup of Goji Berries Dried (40 grams or 1½ oz)
1 Cup/Handful of Papaya (120 grams or 4 oz)
22 grams or ¾ oz of Flax Seeds
150 ml / 5 fl oz of Almond Milk (Unsweetened)

Protein 13g, Fat 13g, Carb 35g, Fibre 12g, 340 Kcals

Preparation

Place the nuts or seeds into the Tall Cup. Screw the Nutribullet Extractor Blade on to the top of the cup. Invert the cup, press it down into the Nutribullet Power Base and twist it into place. Blast them for 30 seconds. Put the rest of the solid ingredients into the cup and press them down below the Max Line. Add the fluid base to fill the cup up to the Max Line. Screw the Nutribullet Extractor Blade on to the top of the cup. Invert the cup, press it down into the Nutribullet Power Base and twist it into place. Blast the mixture until it is really smooth (20 or so seconds). **Enjoy!**

Papaya Paradise

Ingredients

1 Cup/Handful of Black Kale de-stemmed (40 grams or 1½ oz)
1 Cup/Handful of Swiss Chard (40 grams or 1½ oz)
1 Cup/Handful of Apricot halves (120 grams or 4 oz)
1 Cup/Handful of Papaya (120 grams or 4 oz)
22 grams or ¾ oz of Chia Seeds
150 ml / 5 fl oz of Dairy Milk Whole

Protein 13g, Fat 14g, Carb 32g, Fibre 14g, 333 Kcals

Preparation

Place the nuts or seeds into the Tall Cup. Screw the Nutribullet Extractor Blade on to the top of the cup. Invert the cup, press it down into the Nutribullet Power Base and twist it into place. Blast them for 30 seconds. Put the rest of the solid ingredients into the cup and press them down below the Max Line. Add the fluid base to fill the cup up to the Max Line. Screw the Nutribullet Extractor Blade on to the top of the cup. Invert the cup, press it down into the Nutribullet Power Base and twist it into place. Blast the mixture until it is really smooth (20 or so seconds). **Enjoy!**

Spinach needs Almond

Ingredients

1 Cup/Handful of Broccoli Florets (40 grams or 1½ oz)
1 Cup/Handful of Spinach (40 grams or 1½ oz)
1 Cup/Handful of Blueberries (120 grams or 4 oz)
½ Cup of Goji Berries Dried (40 grams or 1½ oz)
30 grams or 1 oz of Almonds
150 ml / 5 fl oz of Almond Milk (Unsweetened)

Protein 16g, Fat 19g, Carb 42g, Fibre 10g, 416 Kcals

Preparation

Place the nuts or seeds into the Tall Cup. Screw the Nutribullet Extractor Blade on to the top of the cup. Invert the cup, press it down into the Nutribullet Power Base and twist it into place. Blast them for 30 seconds. Put the rest of the solid ingredients into the cup and press them down below the Max Line. Add the fluid base to fill the cup up to the Max Line. Screw the Nutribullet Extractor Blade on to the top of the cup. Invert the cup, press it down into the Nutribullet Power Base and twist it into place. Blast the mixture until it is really smooth (20 or so seconds). **Enjoy!**

Raspberry Regatta

Ingredients

1 Cup/Handful of Spinach (40 grams or 1½ oz)
1 Cup/Handful of Black Kale de-stemmed (40 grams or 1½ oz)
1 Cup/Handful of Guava (120 grams or 4 oz)
1 Cup/Handful of Raspberries (120 grams or 4 oz)
22 grams or ¾ oz of Pumpkin Seeds
150 ml / 5 fl oz of Dairy Milk Whole

Protein 17g, Fat 18g, Carb 28g, Fibre 17g, 387 Kcals

Preparation

Place the nuts or seeds into the Tall Cup. Screw the Nutribullet Extractor Blade on to the top of the cup. Invert the cup, press it down into the Nutribullet Power Base and twist it into place. Blast them for 30 seconds. Put the rest of the solid ingredients into the cup and press them down below the Max Line. Add the fluid base to fill the cup up to the Max Line. Screw the Nutribullet Extractor Blade on to the top of the cup. Invert the cup, press it down into the Nutribullet Power Base and twist it into place. Blast the mixture until it is really smooth (20 or so seconds). **Enjoy!**

Avocado on Flax

Ingredients

1 Cup/Handful of Broccoli Florets (40 grams or 1½ oz)
1 Cup/Handful of Swiss Chard (40 grams or 1½ oz)
1 Cup/Handful of Blackberries (120 grams or 4 oz)
1 Cup/Handful of Avocado slices (120 grams or 4 oz)
22 grams or ¾ oz of Flax Seeds
150 ml / 5 fl oz of Almond Milk (Unsweetened)

Protein 11g, Fat 29g, Carb 10g, Fibre 23g, 401 Kcals

Preparation

Place the nuts or seeds into the Tall Cup. Screw the Nutribullet Extractor Blade on to the top of the cup. Invert the cup, press it down into the Nutribullet Power Base and twist it into place. Blast them for 30 seconds. Put the rest of the solid ingredients into the cup and press them down below the Max Line. Add the fluid base to fill the cup up to the Max Line. Screw the Nutribullet Extractor Blade on to the top of the cup. Invert the cup, press it down into the Nutribullet Power Base and twist it into place. Blast the mixture until it is really smooth (20 or so seconds). **Enjoy!**

Blackberry Bliss

Ingredients

1 Cup/Handful of Swiss Chard (40 grams or 1½ oz)
1 Cup/Handful of Broccoli Florets (40 grams or 1½ oz)
1 Cup/Handful of Papaya (120 grams or 4 oz)
1 Cup/Handful of Blackberries (120 grams or 4 oz)
30 grams or 1 oz of Almonds
150 ml / 5 fl oz of Dairy Milk Whole

Protein 15g, Fat 22g, Carb 28g, Fibre 13g, 397 Kcals

Preparation

Place the nuts or seeds into the Tall Cup. Screw the Nutribullet Extractor Blade on to the top of the cup. Invert the cup, press it down into the Nutribullet Power Base and twist it into place. Blast them for 30 seconds. Put the rest of the solid ingredients into the cup and press them down below the Max Line. Add the fluid base to fill the cup up to the Max Line. Screw the Nutribullet Extractor Blade on to the top of the cup. Invert the cup, press it down into the Nutribullet Power Base and twist it into place. Blast the mixture until it is really smooth (20 or so seconds). **Enjoy!**

Goji needs Chia

Ingredients

1 Cup/Handful of Spinach (40 grams or 1½ oz)
1 Cup/Handful of Black Kale de-stemmed (40 grams or 1½ oz)
1 Cup/Handful of Avocado slices (120 grams or 4 oz)
½ Cup of Goji Berries Dried (40 grams or 1½ oz)
22 grams or ¾ oz of Chia Seeds
150 ml / 5 fl oz of Almond Milk (Unsweetened)

Protein 15g, Fat 28g, Carb 28g, Fibre 20g, 470 Kcals

Preparation

Place the nuts or seeds into the Tall Cup. Screw the Nutribullet Extractor Blade on to the top of the cup. Invert the cup, press it down into the Nutribullet Power Base and twist it into place. Blast them for 30 seconds. Put the rest of the solid ingredients into the cup and press them down below the Max Line. Add the fluid base to fill the cup up to the Max Line. Screw the Nutribullet Extractor Blade on to the top of the cup. Invert the cup, press it down into the Nutribullet Power Base and twist it into place. Blast the mixture until it is really smooth (20 or so seconds). **Enjoy!**

Pumpkin Perfection

Ingredients

1 Cup/Handful of Spinach (40 grams or 1½ oz)
1 Cup/Handful of Swiss Chard (40 grams or 1½ oz)
1 Cup/Handful of Apricot halves (120 grams or 4 oz)
1 Cup/Handful of Blueberries (120 grams or 4 oz)
22 grams or ¾ oz of Pumpkin Seeds
150 ml / 5 fl oz of Dairy Milk Whole

Protein 15g, Fat 16g, Carb 36g, Fibre 8g, 363 Kcals

Preparation

Place the nuts or seeds into the Tall Cup. Screw the Nutribullet Extractor Blade on to the top of the cup. Invert the cup, press it down into the Nutribullet Power Base and twist it into place. Blast them for 30 seconds. Put the rest of the solid ingredients into the cup and press them down below the Max Line. Add the fluid base to fill the cup up to the Max Line. Screw the Nutribullet Extractor Blade on to the top of the cup. Invert the cup, press it down into the Nutribullet Power Base and twist it into place. Blast the mixture until it is really smooth (20 or so seconds). **Enjoy!**

Broccoli and Raspberry Mist

Ingredients

1 Cup/Handful of Black Kale de-stemmed (40 grams or 1½ oz)
1 Cup/Handful of Broccoli Florets (40 grams or 1½ oz)
1 Cup/Handful of Guava (120 grams or 4 oz)
1 Cup/Handful of Raspberries (120 grams or 4 oz)
22 grams or ¾ oz of Flax Seeds
150 ml / 5 fl oz of Almond Milk (Unsweetened)

Protein 12g, Fat 14g, Carb 20g, Fibre 23g, 308 Kcals

Preparation

Place the nuts or seeds into the Tall Cup. Screw the Nutribullet Extractor Blade on to the top of the cup. Invert the cup, press it down into the Nutribullet Power Base and twist it into place. Blast them for 30 seconds. Put the rest of the solid ingredients into the cup and press them down below the Max Line. Add the fluid base to fill the cup up to the Max Line. Screw the Nutribullet Extractor Blade on to the top of the cup. Invert the cup, press it down into the Nutribullet Power Base and twist it into place. Blast the mixture until it is really smooth (20 or so seconds). **Enjoy!**

Heart Care Blasts
High in Omega 3

Spinach Supermodel

Ingredients

1 Cup/Handful of Rocket/Arugura Lettuce (40 grams or 1½ oz)
1 Cup/Handful of Spinach (40 grams or 1½ oz)
1 Cup of Strawberries (120 grams or 4 oz)
1 Cup of sliced Tomato (120 grams or 4 oz)
22 grams or ¾ oz of Sesame Seeds Hulled
200 ml / 7 fl oz of Almond Milk (Unsweetened)

Protein 8g, Fat 16g, Carb 12g, Fibre 8g, 232 Kcals

Preparation

Place the nuts or seeds into the Tall Cup. Screw the Nutribullet Extractor Blade on to the top of the cup. Invert the cup, press it down into the Nutribullet Power Base and twist it into place. Blast them for 30 seconds. Put the rest of the solid ingredients into the cup and press them down below the Max Line. Add the fluid base to fill the cup up to the Max Line. Screw the Nutribullet Extractor Blade on to the top of the cup. Invert the cup, press it down into the Nutribullet Power Base and twist it into place. Blast the mixture until it is really smooth (20 or so seconds). **Enjoy!**

Walnut Revision

Ingredients

2 Cups/Handfuls of Broccoli Florets (80 grams or 3 oz)
1 Cup of Nectarine segments (120 grams or 4 oz)
1 Cup of sliced Carrots (120 grams or 4 oz)
30 grams or 1 oz of Walnuts
200 ml / 7 fl oz of Dairy Milk Semi Skimmed

Protein 16g, Fat 24g, Carb 34g, Fibre 9g, 425 Kcals

Preparation

Place the nuts or seeds into the Tall Cup. Screw the Nutribullet Extractor Blade on to the top of the cup. Invert the cup, press it down into the Nutribullet Power Base and twist it into place. Blast them for 30 seconds. Put the rest of the solid ingredients into the cup and press them down below the Max Line. Add the fluid base to fill the cup up to the Max Line. Screw the Nutribullet Extractor Blade on to the top of the cup. Invert the cup, press it down into the Nutribullet Power Base and twist it into place. Blast the mixture until it is really smooth (20 or so seconds). **Enjoy!**

Broccoli Bliss

Ingredients

1 Cup/Handful of Broccoli Florets (40 grams or 1½ oz)
1 Cup/Handful of Lettuce Leaves (40 grams or 1½ oz)
1 Cup of Blackberries (120 grams or 4 oz)
1 Cup of sliced Cauliflower florets (120 grams or 4 oz)
22 grams or ¾ oz of Chia Seeds
200 ml / 7 fl oz of Almond Milk (Unsweetened)

Protein 10g, Fat 10g, Carb 13g, Fibre 19g, 234 Kcals

Preparation

Place the nuts or seeds into the Tall Cup. Screw the Nutribullet Extractor Blade on to the top of the cup. Invert the cup, press it down into the Nutribullet Power Base and twist it into place. Blast them for 30 seconds. Put the rest of the solid ingredients into the cup and press them down below the Max Line. Add the fluid base to fill the cup up to the Max Line. Screw the Nutribullet Extractor Blade on to the top of the cup. Invert the cup, press it down into the Nutribullet Power Base and twist it into place. Blast the mixture until it is really smooth (20 or so seconds). **Enjoy!**

Pecan Perfection

Ingredients

1 Cup/Handful of Rocket/Arugura Lettuce (40 grams or 1½ oz)
1 Cup/Handful of Lettuce Leaves (40 grams or 1½ oz)
1 Cup of Blueberries (120 grams or 4 oz)
1 Cup of sliced Red Pepper (120 grams or 4 oz)
30 grams or 1 oz of Pecans
200 ml / 7 fl oz of Dairy Milk Semi Skimmed

Protein 13g, Fat 26g, Carb 31g, Fibre 10g, 425 Kcals

Preparation

Place the nuts or seeds into the Tall Cup. Screw the Nutribullet Extractor Blade on to the top of the cup. Invert the cup, press it down into the Nutribullet Power Base and twist it into place. Blast them for 30 seconds. Put the rest of the solid ingredients into the cup and press them down below the Max Line. Add the fluid base to fill the cup up to the Max Line. Screw the Nutribullet Extractor Blade on to the top of the cup. Invert the cup, press it down into the Nutribullet Power Base and twist it into place. Blast the mixture until it is really smooth (20 or so seconds). **Enjoy!**

Spinach in Flax

Ingredients

1 Cup/Handful of Broccoli Florets (40 grams or 1½ oz)
1 Cup/Handful of Spinach (40 grams or 1½ oz)
1 Cup of Orange segments (120 grams or 4 oz)
1 Cup of sliced Tomato (120 grams or 4 oz)
22 grams or ¾ oz of Flax Seeds
200 ml / 7 fl oz of Almond Milk (Unsweetened)

Protein 9g, Fat 12g, Carb 17g, Fibre 13g, 244 Kcals

Preparation

Place the nuts or seeds into the Tall Cup. Screw the Nutribullet Extractor Blade on to the top of the cup. Invert the cup, press it down into the Nutribullet Power Base and twist it into place. Blast them for 30 seconds. Put the rest of the solid ingredients into the cup and press them down below the Max Line. Add the fluid base to fill the cup up to the Max Line. Screw the Nutribullet Extractor Blade on to the top of the cup. Invert the cup, press it down into the Nutribullet Power Base and twist it into place. Blast the mixture until it is really smooth (20 or so seconds). **Enjoy!**

Broccoli and Tangerine Dream

Ingredients

1 Cup/Handful of Broccoli Florets (40 grams or 1½ oz)
1 Cup/Handful of Lettuce Leaves (40 grams or 1½ oz)
1 Cup of Tangerine slices (120 grams or 4 oz)
1 Cup of sliced Red Pepper (120 grams or 4 oz)
30 grams or 1 oz of Pecans
200 ml / 7 fl oz of Dairy Milk Semi Skimmed

Protein 14g, Fat 26g, Carb 32g, Fibre 9g, 428 Kcals

Preparation

Place the nuts or seeds into the Tall Cup. Screw the Nutribullet Extractor Blade on to the top of the cup. Invert the cup, press it down into the Nutribullet Power Base and twist it into place. Blast them for 30 seconds. Put the rest of the solid ingredients into the cup and press them down below the Max Line. Add the fluid base to fill the cup up to the Max Line. Screw the Nutribullet Extractor Blade on to the top of the cup. Invert the cup, press it down into the Nutribullet Power Base and twist it into place. Blast the mixture until it is really smooth (20 or so seconds). **Enjoy!**

Flax Fusion

Ingredients

2 Cups/Handfuls of Spinach (80 grams or 3 oz)
1 Cup of Guava (120 grams or 4 oz)
1 Cup of sliced Cauliflower florets (120 grams or 4 oz)
22 grams or ¾ oz of Flax Seeds
200 ml / 7 fl oz of Almond Milk (Unsweetened)

Protein 13g, Fat 13g, Carb 16g, Fibre 17g, 273 Kcals

Preparation

Place the nuts or seeds into the Tall Cup. Screw the Nutribullet Extractor Blade on to the top of the cup. Invert the cup, press it down into the Nutribullet Power Base and twist it into place. Blast them for 30 seconds. Put the rest of the solid ingredients into the cup and press them down below the Max Line. Add the fluid base to fill the cup up to the Max Line. Screw the Nutribullet Extractor Blade on to the top of the cup. Invert the cup, press it down into the Nutribullet Power Base and twist it into place. Blast the mixture until it is really smooth (20 or so seconds). **Enjoy!**

Spinach and Walnut Elixir

Ingredients

1 Cup/Handful of Rocket/Arugura Lettuce (40 grams or 1½ oz)
1 Cup/Handful of Spinach (40 grams or 1½ oz)
1 Cup of Raspberries (120 grams or 4 oz)
1 Cup of sliced Carrots (120 grams or 4 oz)
30 grams or 1 oz of Walnuts
200 ml / 7 fl oz of Dairy Milk Semi Skimmed

Protein 16g, Fat 24g, Carb 28g, Fibre 15g, 422 Kcals

Preparation

Place the nuts or seeds into the Tall Cup. Screw the Nutribullet Extractor Blade on to the top of the cup. Invert the cup, press it down into the Nutribullet Power Base and twist it into place. Blast them for 30 seconds. Put the rest of the solid ingredients into the cup and press them down below the Max Line. Add the fluid base to fill the cup up to the Max Line. Screw the Nutribullet Extractor Blade on to the top of the cup. Invert the cup, press it down into the Nutribullet Power Base and twist it into place. Blast the mixture until it is really smooth (20 or so seconds). **Enjoy!**

Blackberry loves Tomato

Ingredients

1 Cup/Handful of Broccoli Florets (40 grams or 1½ oz)
1 Cup/Handful of Spinach (40 grams or 1½ oz)
1 Cup of Blackberries (120 grams or 4 oz)
1 Cup of sliced Tomato (120 grams or 4 oz)
22 grams or ¾ oz of Sesame Seeds Hulled
200 ml / 7 fl oz of Dairy Milk Semi Skimmed

Protein 16g, Fat 17g, Carb 20g, Fibre 11g, 327 Kcals

Preparation

Place the nuts or seeds into the Tall Cup. Screw the Nutribullet Extractor Blade on to the top of the cup. Invert the cup, press it down into the Nutribullet Power Base and twist it into place. Blast them for 30 seconds. Put the rest of the solid ingredients into the cup and press them down below the Max Line. Add the fluid base to fill the cup up to the Max Line. Screw the Nutribullet Extractor Blade on to the top of the cup. Invert the cup, press it down into the Nutribullet Power Base and twist it into place. Blast the mixture until it is really smooth (20 or so seconds). **Enjoy!**

Lettuce embraces Chia

Ingredients

1 Cup/Handful of Lettuce Leaves (40 grams or 1½ oz)
1 Cup/Handful of Rocket/Arugura Lettuce (40 grams or 1½ oz)
1 Cup of Nectarine segments (120 grams or 4 oz)
1 Cup of sliced Red Pepper (120 grams or 4 oz)
22 grams or ¾ oz of Chia Seeds
200 ml / 7 fl oz of Almond Milk (Unsweetened)

Protein 8g, Fat 10g, Carb 18g, Fibre 14g, 235 Kcals

Preparation

Place the nuts or seeds into the Tall Cup. Screw the Nutribullet Extractor Blade on to the top of the cup. Invert the cup, press it down into the Nutribullet Power Base and twist it into place. Blast them for 30 seconds. Put the rest of the solid ingredients into the cup and press them down below the Max Line. Add the fluid base to fill the cup up to the Max Line. Screw the Nutribullet Extractor Blade on to the top of the cup. Invert the cup, press it down into the Nutribullet Power Base and twist it into place. Blast the mixture until it is really smooth (20 or so seconds). **Enjoy!**

Carrot Cornucopia

Ingredients

1 Cup/Handful of Rocket/Arugura Lettuce (40 grams or 1½ oz)
1 Cup/Handful of Lettuce Leaves (40 grams or 1½ oz)
1 Cup of Guava (120 grams or 4 oz)
1 Cup of sliced Carrots (120 grams or 4 oz)
30 grams or 1 oz of Walnuts
200 ml / 7 fl oz of Dairy Milk Semi Skimmed

Protein 17g, Fat 25g, Carb 32g, Fibre 13g, 439 Kcals

Preparation

Place the nuts or seeds into the Tall Cup. Screw the Nutribullet Extractor Blade on to the top of the cup. Invert the cup, press it down into the Nutribullet Power Base and twist it into place. Blast them for 30 seconds. Put the rest of the solid ingredients into the cup and press them down below the Max Line. Add the fluid base to fill the cup up to the Max Line. Screw the Nutribullet Extractor Blade on to the top of the cup. Invert the cup, press it down into the Nutribullet Power Base and twist it into place. Blast the mixture until it is really smooth (20 or so seconds). **Enjoy!**

Spinach on Blueberry

Ingredients

1 Cup/Handful of Broccoli Florets (40 grams or 1½ oz)
1 Cup/Handful of Spinach (40 grams or 1½ oz)
1 Cup of Blueberries (120 grams or 4 oz)
1 Cup of sliced Cauliflower florets (120 grams or 4 oz)
30 grams or 1 oz of Pecans
200 ml / 7 fl oz of Almond Milk (Unsweetened)

Protein 9g, Fat 25g, Carb 22g, Fibre 11g, 354 Kcals

Preparation

Place the nuts or seeds into the Tall Cup. Screw the Nutribullet Extractor Blade on to the top of the cup. Invert the cup, press it down into the Nutribullet Power Base and twist it into place. Blast them for 30 seconds. Put the rest of the solid ingredients into the cup and press them down below the Max Line. Add the fluid base to fill the cup up to the Max Line. Screw the Nutribullet Extractor Blade on to the top of the cup. Invert the cup, press it down into the Nutribullet Power Base and twist it into place. Blast the mixture until it is really smooth (20 or so seconds). **Enjoy!**

Rocket Mirage

Ingredients

2 Cups/Handfuls of Rocket/Arugura Lettuce (80 grams or 3 oz)
1 Cup of Raspberries (120 grams or 4 oz)
1 Cup of sliced Carrots (120 grams or 4 oz)
22 grams or ¾ oz of Sesame Seeds Hulled
200 ml / 7 fl oz of Dairy Milk Semi Skimmed

Protein 15g, Fat 18g, Carb 26g, Fibre 14g, 355 Kcals

Preparation

Place the nuts or seeds into the Tall Cup. Screw the Nutribullet Extractor Blade on to the top of the cup. Invert the cup, press it down into the Nutribullet Power Base and twist it into place. Blast them for 30 seconds. Put the rest of the solid ingredients into the cup and press them down below the Max Line. Add the fluid base to fill the cup up to the Max Line. Screw the Nutribullet Extractor Blade on to the top of the cup. Invert the cup, press it down into the Nutribullet Power Base and twist it into place. Blast the mixture until it is really smooth (20 or so seconds). **Enjoy!**

Spinach meets Orange

Ingredients

1 Cup/Handful of Spinach (40 grams or 1½ oz)
1 Cup/Handful of Lettuce Leaves (40 grams or 1½ oz)
1 Cup of Orange segments (120 grams or 4 oz)
1 Cup of sliced Cauliflower florets (120 grams or 4 oz)
22 grams or ¾ oz of Chia Seeds
200 ml / 7 fl oz of Dairy Milk Semi Skimmed

Protein 16g, Fat 11g, Carb 27g, Fibre 15g, 309 Kcals

Preparation

Place the nuts or seeds into the Tall Cup. Screw the Nutribullet Extractor Blade on to the top of the cup. Invert the cup, press it down into the Nutribullet Power Base and twist it into place. Blast them for 30 seconds. Put the rest of the solid ingredients into the cup and press them down below the Max Line. Add the fluid base to fill the cup up to the Max Line. Screw the Nutribullet Extractor Blade on to the top of the cup. Invert the cup, press it down into the Nutribullet Power Base and twist it into place. Blast the mixture until it is really smooth (20 or so seconds). **Enjoy!**

Broccoli and Nectarine Delight

Ingredients

1 Cup/Handful of Rocket/Arugura Lettuce (40 grams or 1½ oz)
1 Cup/Handful of Broccoli Florets (40 grams or 1½ oz)
1 Cup of Nectarine segments (120 grams or 4 oz)
1 Cup of sliced Carrots (120 grams or 4 oz)
22 grams or ¾ oz of Sesame Seeds Hulled
200 ml / 7 fl oz of Dairy Milk Semi Skimmed

Protein 15g, Fat 17g, Carb 31g, Fibre 9g, 353 Kcals

Preparation

Place the nuts or seeds into the Tall Cup. Screw the Nutribullet Extractor Blade on to the top of the cup. Invert the cup, press it down into the Nutribullet Power Base and twist it into place. Blast them for 30 seconds. Put the rest of the solid ingredients into the cup and press them down below the Max Line. Add the fluid base to fill the cup up to the Max Line. Screw the Nutribullet Extractor Blade on to the top of the cup. Invert the cup, press it down into the Nutribullet Power Base and twist it into place. Blast the mixture until it is really smooth (20 or so seconds). **Enjoy!**

Red Pepper Reaction

Ingredients

1 Cup/Handful of Broccoli Florets (40 grams or 1½ oz)
1 Cup/Handful of Spinach (40 grams or 1½ oz)
1 Cup of Tangerine slices (120 grams or 4 oz)
1 Cup of sliced Red Pepper (120 grams or 4 oz)
30 grams or 1 oz of Walnuts
200 ml / 7 fl oz of Almond Milk (Unsweetened)

Protein 10g, Fat 23g, Carb 23g, Fibre 9g, 345 Kcals

Preparation

Place the nuts or seeds into the Tall Cup. Screw the Nutribullet Extractor Blade on to the top of the cup. Invert the cup, press it down into the Nutribullet Power Base and twist it into place. Blast them for 30 seconds. Put the rest of the solid ingredients into the cup and press them down below the Max Line. Add the fluid base to fill the cup up to the Max Line. Screw the Nutribullet Extractor Blade on to the top of the cup. Invert the cup, press it down into the Nutribullet Power Base and twist it into place. Blast the mixture until it is really smooth (20 or so seconds). **Enjoy!**

Rocket and Orange Opera

Ingredients

1 Cup/Handful of Rocket/Arugura Lettuce (40 grams or 1½ oz)
1 Cup/Handful of Lettuce Leaves (40 grams or 1½ oz)
1 Cup of Orange segments (120 grams or 4 oz)
1 Cup of sliced Tomato (120 grams or 4 oz)
30 grams or 1 oz of Pecans
200 ml / 7 fl oz of Dairy Milk Semi Skimmed

Protein 13g, Fat 26g, Carb 26g, Fibre 9g, 398 Kcals

Preparation

Place the nuts or seeds into the Tall Cup. Screw the Nutribullet Extractor Blade on to the top of the cup. Invert the cup, press it down into the Nutribullet Power Base and twist it into place. Blast them for 30 seconds. Put the rest of the solid ingredients into the cup and press them down below the Max Line. Add the fluid base to fill the cup up to the Max Line. Screw the Nutribullet Extractor Blade on to the top of the cup. Invert the cup, press it down into the Nutribullet Power Base and twist it into place. Blast the mixture until it is really smooth (20 or so seconds). **Enjoy!**

Raspberry Recovery

Ingredients

1 Cup/Handful of Broccoli Florets (40 grams or 1½ oz)
1 Cup/Handful of Rocket/Arugura Lettuce (40 grams or 1½ oz)
1 Cup of Raspberries (120 grams or 4 oz)
1 Cup of sliced Cauliflower florets (120 grams or 4 oz)
22 grams or ¾ oz of Flax Seeds
200 ml / 7 fl oz of Almond Milk (Unsweetened)

Protein 10g, Fat 13g, Carb 13g, Fibre 19g, 255 Kcals

Preparation

Place the nuts or seeds into the Tall Cup. Screw the Nutribullet Extractor Blade on to the top of the cup. Invert the cup, press it down into the Nutribullet Power Base and twist it into place. Blast them for 30 seconds. Put the rest of the solid ingredients into the cup and press them down below the Max Line. Add the fluid base to fill the cup up to the Max Line. Screw the Nutribullet Extractor Blade on to the top of the cup. Invert the cup, press it down into the Nutribullet Power Base and twist it into place. Blast the mixture until it is really smooth (20 or so seconds). **Enjoy!**

Broccoli goes Blackberry

Ingredients

2 Cups/Handfuls of Broccoli Florets (80 grams or 3 oz)
1 Cup of Blackberries (120 grams or 4 oz)
1 Cup of sliced Carrots (120 grams or 4 oz)
30 grams or 1 oz of Pecans
200 ml / 7 fl oz of Dairy Milk Semi Skimmed

Protein 15g, Fat 26g, Carb 27g, Fibre 15g, 435 Kcals

Preparation

Place the nuts or seeds into the Tall Cup. Screw the Nutribullet Extractor Blade on to the top of the cup. Invert the cup, press it down into the Nutribullet Power Base and twist it into place. Blast them for 30 seconds. Put the rest of the solid ingredients into the cup and press them down below the Max Line. Add the fluid base to fill the cup up to the Max Line. Screw the Nutribullet Extractor Blade on to the top of the cup. Invert the cup, press it down into the Nutribullet Power Base and twist it into place. Blast the mixture until it is really smooth (20 or so seconds). **Enjoy!**

Lettuce and Guava Panacea

Ingredients

1 Cup/Handful of Spinach (40 grams or 1½ oz)
1 Cup/Handful of Lettuce Leaves (40 grams or 1½ oz)
1 Cup of Guava (120 grams or 4 oz)
1 Cup of sliced Red Pepper (120 grams or 4 oz)
22 grams or ¾ oz of Sesame Seeds Hulled
200 ml / 7 fl oz of Almond Milk (Unsweetened)

Protein 11g, Fat 17g, Carb 17g, Fibre 13g, 292 Kcals

Preparation

Place the nuts or seeds into the Tall Cup. Screw the Nutribullet Extractor Blade on to the top of the cup. Invert the cup, press it down into the Nutribullet Power Base and twist it into place. Blast them for 30 seconds. Put the rest of the solid ingredients into the cup and press them down below the Max Line. Add the fluid base to fill the cup up to the Max Line. Screw the Nutribullet Extractor Blade on to the top of the cup. Invert the cup, press it down into the Nutribullet Power Base and twist it into place. Blast the mixture until it is really smooth (20 or so seconds). **Enjoy!**

Happiness, Deep Sleep and Stress Busting Blasts
High in Tryptophan, Magnesium, Vit B3, B6, B9

Carrot Constellation

Ingredients

1 Cup/Handful of Broccoli Florets (40 grams or 1½ oz)
1 Cup/Handful of Watercress (40 grams or 1½ oz)
1 Cup of Apricot halves (120 grams or 4 oz)
1 Cup of sliced Carrots (120 grams or 4 oz)
22 grams or ¾ oz of Pumpkin Seeds
200 ml / 7 fl oz of Almond Milk (Unsweetened)

Protein 11g, Fat 13g, Carb 23g, Fibre 9g, 275 Kcals

Preparation

Place the nuts or seeds into the Tall Cup. Screw the Nutribullet Extractor Blade on to the top of the cup. Invert the cup, press it down into the Nutribullet Power Base and twist it into place. Blast them for 30 seconds. Put the rest of the solid ingredients into the cup and press them down below the Max Line. Add the fluid base to fill the cup up to the Max Line. Screw the Nutribullet Extractor Blade on to the top of the cup. Invert the cup, press it down into the Nutribullet Power Base and twist it into place. Blast the mixture until it is really smooth (20 or so seconds). **Enjoy!**

Watercress and Avocado Invigorator

Ingredients

2 Cups/Handfuls of Watercress (80 grams or 3 oz)
1 small Avocado (stoned and peeled) (120 grams or 4 oz)
1 Cup of sliced Cauliflower florets (120 grams or 4 oz)
22 grams or ¾ oz of Chia Seeds
200 ml / 7 fl oz of Dairy Milk Semi Skimmed

Protein 17g, Fat 28g, Carb 18g, Fibre 18g, 437 Kcals

Preparation

Place the nuts or seeds into the Tall Cup. Screw the Nutribullet Extractor Blade on to the top of the cup. Invert the cup, press it down into the Nutribullet Power Base and twist it into place. Blast them for 30 seconds. Put the rest of the solid ingredients into the cup and press them down below the Max Line. Add the fluid base to fill the cup up to the Max Line. Screw the Nutribullet Extractor Blade on to the top of the cup. Invert the cup, press it down into the Nutribullet Power Base and twist it into place. Blast the mixture until it is really smooth (20 or so seconds). **Enjoy!**

Prune and Beetroot Kiss

Ingredients

1 Cup/Handful of Spinach (40 grams or 1½ oz)
1 Cup/Handful of Broccoli Florets (40 grams or 1½ oz)
1 Cup of Prunes (stoned) (120 grams or 4 oz)
1 Cup of diced Beetroot (120 grams or 4 oz)
30 grams or 1 oz of Peanuts
200 ml / 7 fl oz of Dairy Milk Semi Skimmed

Protein 20g, Fat 21g, Carb 26g, Fibre 11g, 349 Kcals

Preparation

Place the nuts or seeds into the Tall Cup. Screw the Nutribullet Extractor Blade on to the top of the cup. Invert the cup, press it down into the Nutribullet Power Base and twist it into place. Blast them for 30 seconds. Put the rest of the solid ingredients into the cup and press them down below the Max Line. Add the fluid base to fill the cup up to the Max Line. Screw the Nutribullet Extractor Blade on to the top of the cup. Invert the cup, press it down into the Nutribullet Power Base and twist it into place. Blast the mixture until it is really smooth (20 or so seconds). **Enjoy!**

Broccoli and Sunflower Garden

Ingredients

2 Cups/Handfuls of Broccoli Florets (80 grams or 3 oz)
1 Cup of Apricot halves (120 grams or 4 oz)
1 Cup of sliced Fine Beans (120 grams or 4 oz)
22 grams or ¾ oz of Sunflower Seeds Hulled
200 ml / 7 fl oz of Almond Milk (Unsweetened)

Protein 11g, Fat 14g, Carb 21g, Fibre 9g, 254 Kcals

Preparation

Place the nuts or seeds into the Tall Cup. Screw the Nutribullet Extractor Blade on to the top of the cup. Invert the cup, press it down into the Nutribullet Power Base and twist it into place. Blast them for 30 seconds. Put the rest of the solid ingredients into the cup and press them down below the Max Line. Add the fluid base to fill the cup up to the Max Line. Screw the Nutribullet Extractor Blade on to the top of the cup. Invert the cup, press it down into the Nutribullet Power Base and twist it into place. Blast the mixture until it is really smooth (20 or so seconds). **Enjoy!**

Prune Panache

Ingredients

2 Cups/Handfuls of Watercress (80 grams or 3 oz)
1 Cup of Prunes (stoned) (120 grams or 4 oz)
1 Cup of sliced Carrots (120 grams or 4 oz)
22 grams or ¾ oz of Sesame Seeds Hulled
200 ml / 7 fl oz of Almond Milk (Unsweetened)

Protein 9g, Fat 17g, Carb 13g, Fibre 9g, 220 Kcals

Preparation

Place the nuts or seeds into the Tall Cup. Screw the Nutribullet Extractor Blade on to the top of the cup. Invert the cup, press it down into the Nutribullet Power Base and twist it into place. Blast them for 30 seconds. Put the rest of the solid ingredients into the cup and press them down below the Max Line. Add the fluid base to fill the cup up to the Max Line. Screw the Nutribullet Extractor Blade on to the top of the cup. Invert the cup, press it down into the Nutribullet Power Base and twist it into place. Blast the mixture until it is really smooth (20 or so seconds). **Enjoy!**

Spinach and Cashew Cascade

Ingredients

1 Cup/Handful of Watercress (40 grams or 1½ oz)
1 Cup/Handful of Spinach (40 grams or 1½ oz)
1 small Avocado (stoned and peeled) (120 grams or 4 oz)
1 Cup of diced Beetroot (120 grams or 4 oz)
30 grams or 1 oz of Cashews
200 ml / 7 fl oz of Dairy Milk Semi Skimmed

Protein 19g, Fat 35g, Carb 29g, Fibre 13g, 523 Kcals

Preparation

Place the nuts or seeds into the Tall Cup. Screw the Nutribullet Extractor Blade on to the top of the cup. Invert the cup, press it down into the Nutribullet Power Base and twist it into place. Blast them for 30 seconds. Put the rest of the solid ingredients into the cup and press them down below the Max Line. Add the fluid base to fill the cup up to the Max Line. Screw the Nutribullet Extractor Blade on to the top of the cup. Invert the cup, press it down into the Nutribullet Power Base and twist it into place. Blast the mixture until it is really smooth (20 or so seconds). **Enjoy!**

Watercress Waistline

Ingredients

1 Cup/Handful of Broccoli Florets (40 grams or 1½ oz)
1 Cup/Handful of Watercress (40 grams or 1½ oz)
1 Cup of Apricot halves (120 grams or 4 oz)
1 Cup of sliced Fine Beans (120 grams or 4 oz)
30 grams or 1 oz of Walnuts
200 ml / 7 fl oz of Almond Milk (Unsweetened)

Protein 11g, Fat 23g, Carb 19g, Fibre 9g, 327 Kcals

Preparation

Place the nuts or seeds into the Tall Cup. Screw the Nutribullet Extractor Blade on to the top of the cup. Invert the cup, press it down into the Nutribullet Power Base and twist it into place. Blast them for 30 seconds. Put the rest of the solid ingredients into the cup and press them down below the Max Line. Add the fluid base to fill the cup up to the Max Line. Screw the Nutribullet Extractor Blade on to the top of the cup. Invert the cup, press it down into the Nutribullet Power Base and twist it into place. Blast the mixture until it is really smooth (20 or so seconds). **Enjoy!**

Spinach joins Avocado

Ingredients

1 Cup/Handful of Spinach (40 grams or 1½ oz)
1 Cup/Handful of Broccoli Florets (40 grams or 1½ oz)
1 small Avocado (stoned and peeled) (120 grams or 4 oz)
1 Cup of sliced Cauliflower florets (120 grams or 4 oz)
30 grams or 1 oz of Walnuts
200 ml / 7 fl oz of Dairy Milk Semi Skimmed

Protein 19g, Fat 41g, Carb 20g, Fibre 14g, 540 Kcals

Preparation

Place the nuts or seeds into the Tall Cup. Screw the Nutribullet Extractor Blade on to the top of the cup. Invert the cup, press it down into the Nutribullet Power Base and twist it into place. Blast them for 30 seconds. Put the rest of the solid ingredients into the cup and press them down below the Max Line. Add the fluid base to fill the cup up to the Max Line. Screw the Nutribullet Extractor Blade on to the top of the cup. Invert the cup, press it down into the Nutribullet Power Base and twist it into place. Blast the mixture until it is really smooth (20 or so seconds). **Enjoy!**

Watercress goes Spinach

Ingredients

1 Cup/Handful of Watercress (40 grams or 1½ oz)
1 Cup/Handful of Spinach (40 grams or 1½ oz)
1 Cup of Prunes (stoned) (120 grams or 4 oz)
1 Cup of sliced Fine Beans (120 grams or 4 oz)
22 grams or ¾ oz of Pumpkin Seeds
200 ml / 7 fl oz of Dairy Milk Semi Skimmed

Protein 18g, Fat 16g, Carb 20g, Fibre 8g, 272 Kcals

Preparation

Place the nuts or seeds into the Tall Cup. Screw the Nutribullet Extractor Blade on to the top of the cup. Invert the cup, press it down into the Nutribullet Power Base and twist it into place. Blast them for 30 seconds. Put the rest of the solid ingredients into the cup and press them down below the Max Line. Add the fluid base to fill the cup up to the Max Line. Screw the Nutribullet Extractor Blade on to the top of the cup. Invert the cup, press it down into the Nutribullet Power Base and twist it into place. Blast the mixture until it is really smooth (20 or so seconds). **Enjoy!**

Broccoli embraces Peanut

Ingredients

1 Cup/Handful of Broccoli Florets (40 grams or 1½ oz)
1 Cup/Handful of Spinach (40 grams or 1½ oz)
1 small Avocado (stoned and peeled) (120 grams or 4 oz)
1 Cup of sliced Carrots (120 grams or 4 oz)
30 grams or 1 oz of Peanuts
200 ml / 7 fl oz of Almond Milk (Unsweetened)

Protein 14g, Fat 35g, Carb 15g, Fibre 17g, 460 Kcals

Preparation

Place the nuts or seeds into the Tall Cup. Screw the Nutribullet Extractor Blade on to the top of the cup. Invert the cup, press it down into the Nutribullet Power Base and twist it into place. Blast them for 30 seconds. Put the rest of the solid ingredients into the cup and press them down below the Max Line. Add the fluid base to fill the cup up to the Max Line. Screw the Nutribullet Extractor Blade on to the top of the cup. Invert the cup, press it down into the Nutribullet Power Base and twist it into place. Blast the mixture until it is really smooth (20 or so seconds). **Enjoy!**

Prune and Cauliflower Ensemble

Ingredients

1 Cup/Handful of Watercress (40 grams or 1½ oz)
1 Cup/Handful of Spinach (40 grams or 1½ oz)
1 Cup of Prunes (stoned) (120 grams or 4 oz)
1 Cup of sliced Cauliflower florets (120 grams or 4 oz)
22 grams or ¾ oz of Chia Seeds
200 ml / 7 fl oz of Dairy Milk Semi Skimmed

Protein 16g, Fat 13g, Carb 20g, Fibre 14g, 255 Kcals

Preparation

Place the nuts or seeds into the Tall Cup. Screw the Nutribullet Extractor Blade on to the top of the cup. Invert the cup, press it down into the Nutribullet Power Base and twist it into place. Blast them for 30 seconds. Put the rest of the solid ingredients into the cup and press them down below the Max Line. Add the fluid base to fill the cup up to the Max Line. Screw the Nutribullet Extractor Blade on to the top of the cup. Invert the cup, press it down into the Nutribullet Power Base and twist it into place. Blast the mixture until it is really smooth (20 or so seconds). **Enjoy!**

Broccoli Morning

Ingredients

1 Cup/Handful of Watercress (40 grams or 1½ oz)
1 Cup/Handful of Broccoli Florets (40 grams or 1½ oz)
1 Cup of Apricot halves (120 grams or 4 oz)
1 Cup of diced Beetroot (120 grams or 4 oz)
22 grams or ¾ oz of Sesame Seeds Hulled
200 ml / 7 fl oz of Almond Milk (Unsweetened)

Protein 10g, Fat 16g, Carb 21g, Fibre 10g, 284 Kcals

Preparation

Place the nuts or seeds into the Tall Cup. Screw the Nutribullet Extractor Blade on to the top of the cup. Invert the cup, press it down into the Nutribullet Power Base and twist it into place. Blast them for 30 seconds. Put the rest of the solid ingredients into the cup and press them down below the Max Line. Add the fluid base to fill the cup up to the Max Line. Screw the Nutribullet Extractor Blade on to the top of the cup. Invert the cup, press it down into the Nutribullet Power Base and twist it into place. Blast the mixture until it is really smooth (20 or so seconds). **Enjoy!**

Spinach Heaven

Ingredients

1 Cup/Handful of Spinach (40 grams or 1½ oz)
1 Cup/Handful of Watercress (40 grams or 1½ oz)
1 Cup of Prunes (stoned) (120 grams or 4 oz)
1 Cup of sliced Carrots (120 grams or 4 oz)
22 grams or ¾ oz of Sesame Seeds Hulled
200 ml / 7 fl oz of Almond Milk (Unsweetened)

Protein 9g, Fat 17g, Carb 13g, Fibre 10g, 225 Kcals

Preparation

Place the nuts or seeds into the Tall Cup. Screw the Nutribullet Extractor Blade on to the top of the cup. Invert the cup, press it down into the Nutribullet Power Base and twist it into place. Blast them for 30 seconds. Put the rest of the solid ingredients into the cup and press them down below the Max Line. Add the fluid base to fill the cup up to the Max Line. Screw the Nutribullet Extractor Blade on to the top of the cup. Invert the cup, press it down into the Nutribullet Power Base and twist it into place. Blast the mixture until it is really smooth (20 or so seconds). **Enjoy!**

Pumpkin Power

Ingredients

2 Cups/Handfuls of Spinach (80 grams or 3 oz)
1 small Avocado (stoned and peeled) (120 grams or 4 oz)
1 Cup of sliced Fine Beans (120 grams or 4 oz)
22 grams or ¾ oz of Pumpkin Seeds
200 ml / 7 fl oz of Dairy Milk Semi Skimmed

Protein 19g, Fat 32g, Carb 19g, Fibre 14g, 464 Kcals

Preparation

Place the nuts or seeds into the Tall Cup. Screw the Nutribullet Extractor Blade on to the top of the cup. Invert the cup, press it down into the Nutribullet Power Base and twist it into place. Blast them for 30 seconds. Put the rest of the solid ingredients into the cup and press them down below the Max Line. Add the fluid base to fill the cup up to the Max Line. Screw the Nutribullet Extractor Blade on to the top of the cup. Invert the cup, press it down into the Nutribullet Power Base and twist it into place. Blast the mixture until it is really smooth (20 or so seconds). **Enjoy!**

Apricot finds Beetroot

Ingredients

1 Cup/Handful of Spinach (40 grams or 1½ oz)
1 Cup/Handful of Broccoli Florets (40 grams or 1½ oz)
1 Cup of Apricot halves (120 grams or 4 oz)
1 Cup of diced Beetroot (120 grams or 4 oz)
30 grams or 1 oz of Peanuts
200 ml / 7 fl oz of Dairy Milk Semi Skimmed

Protein 21g, Fat 19g, Carb 33g, Fibre 10g, 402 Kcals

Preparation

Place the nuts or seeds into the Tall Cup. Screw the Nutribullet Extractor Blade on to the top of the cup. Invert the cup, press it down into the Nutribullet Power Base and twist it into place. Blast them for 30 seconds. Put the rest of the solid ingredients into the cup and press them down below the Max Line. Add the fluid base to fill the cup up to the Max Line. Screw the Nutribullet Extractor Blade on to the top of the cup. Invert the cup, press it down into the Nutribullet Power Base and twist it into place. Blast the mixture until it is really smooth (20 or so seconds). **Enjoy!**

Chia Collection

Ingredients

1 Cup/Handful of Broccoli Florets (40 grams or 1½ oz)
1 Cup/Handful of Spinach (40 grams or 1½ oz)
1 Cup of Prunes (stoned) (120 grams or 4 oz)
1 Cup of sliced Carrots (120 grams or 4 oz)
22 grams or ¾ oz of Chia Seeds
200 ml / 7 fl oz of Almond Milk (Unsweetened)

Protein 9g, Fat 12g, Carb 16g, Fibre 17g, 209 Kcals

Preparation

Place the nuts or seeds into the Tall Cup. Screw the Nutribullet Extractor Blade on to the top of the cup. Invert the cup, press it down into the Nutribullet Power Base and twist it into place. Blast them for 30 seconds. Put the rest of the solid ingredients into the cup and press them down below the Max Line. Add the fluid base to fill the cup up to the Max Line. Screw the Nutribullet Extractor Blade on to the top of the cup. Invert the cup, press it down into the Nutribullet Power Base and twist it into place. Blast the mixture until it is really smooth (20 or so seconds). **Enjoy!**

Sunflower Blossom

Ingredients

1 Cup/Handful of Watercress (40 grams or 1½ oz)
1 Cup/Handful of Broccoli Florets (40 grams or 1½ oz)
1 small Avocado (stoned and peeled) (120 grams or 4 oz)
1 Cup of sliced Fine Beans (120 grams or 4 oz)
22 grams or ¾ oz of Sunflower Seeds Hulled
200 ml / 7 fl oz of Dairy Milk Semi Skimmed

Protein 18g, Fat 32g, Carb 20g, Fibre 13g, 453 Kcals

Preparation

Place the nuts or seeds into the Tall Cup. Screw the Nutribullet Extractor Blade on to the top of the cup. Invert the cup, press it down into the Nutribullet Power Base and twist it into place. Blast them for 30 seconds. Put the rest of the solid ingredients into the cup and press them down below the Max Line. Add the fluid base to fill the cup up to the Max Line. Screw the Nutribullet Extractor Blade on to the top of the cup. Invert the cup, press it down into the Nutribullet Power Base and twist it into place. Blast the mixture until it is really smooth (20 or so seconds). **Enjoy!**

Apricot Debut

Ingredients

2 Cups/Handfuls of Watercress (80 grams or 3 oz)
1 Cup of Apricot halves (120 grams or 4 oz)
1 Cup of sliced Cauliflower florets (120 grams or 4 oz)
22 grams or ¾ oz of Chia Seeds
200 ml / 7 fl oz of Almond Milk (Unsweetened)

Protein 10g, Fat 10g, Carb 17g, Fibre 14g, 229 Kcals

Preparation

Place the nuts or seeds into the Tall Cup. Screw the Nutribullet Extractor Blade on to the top of the cup. Invert the cup, press it down into the Nutribullet Power Base and twist it into place. Blast them for 30 seconds. Put the rest of the solid ingredients into the cup and press them down below the Max Line. Add the fluid base to fill the cup up to the Max Line. Screw the Nutribullet Extractor Blade on to the top of the cup. Invert the cup, press it down into the Nutribullet Power Base and twist it into place. Blast the mixture until it is really smooth (20 or so seconds). **Enjoy!**

Watercress and Sesame Mist

Ingredients

1 Cup/Handful of Spinach (40 grams or 1½ oz)
1 Cup/Handful of Watercress (40 grams or 1½ oz)
1 Cup of Prunes (stoned) (120 grams or 4 oz)
1 Cup of diced Beetroot (120 grams or 4 oz)
22 grams or ¾ oz of Sesame Seeds Hulled
200 ml / 7 fl oz of Almond Milk (Unsweetened)

Protein 10g, Fat 17g, Carb 13g, Fibre 10g, 227 Kcals

Preparation

Place the nuts or seeds into the Tall Cup. Screw the Nutribullet Extractor Blade on to the top of the cup. Invert the cup, press it down into the Nutribullet Power Base and twist it into place. Blast them for 30 seconds. Put the rest of the solid ingredients into the cup and press them down below the Max Line. Add the fluid base to fill the cup up to the Max Line. Screw the Nutribullet Extractor Blade on to the top of the cup. Invert the cup, press it down into the Nutribullet Power Base and twist it into place. Blast the mixture until it is really smooth (20 or so seconds). **Enjoy!**

Avocado Anthem

Ingredients

1 Cup/Handful of Broccoli Florets (40 grams or 1½ oz)
1 Cup/Handful of Watercress (40 grams or 1½ oz)
1 small Avocado (stoned and peeled) (120 grams or 4 oz)
1 Cup of sliced Carrots (120 grams or 4 oz)
30 grams or 1 oz of Walnuts
200 ml / 7 fl oz of Dairy Milk Semi Skimmed

Protein 17g, Fat 41g, Carb 24g, Fibre 15g, 555 Kcals

Preparation

Place the nuts or seeds into the Tall Cup. Screw the Nutribullet Extractor Blade on to the top of the cup. Invert the cup, press it down into the Nutribullet Power Base and twist it into place. Blast them for 30 seconds. Put the rest of the solid ingredients into the cup and press them down below the Max Line. Add the fluid base to fill the cup up to the Max Line. Screw the Nutribullet Extractor Blade on to the top of the cup. Invert the cup, press it down into the Nutribullet Power Base and twist it into place. Blast the mixture until it is really smooth (20 or so seconds). **Enjoy!**

Classic Desserts

Raspberry in Walnut

Ingredients

2 Cups of Raspberries (240 grams or 8 oz)
30 grams or 1 oz of Walnuts
200 ml / 7 fl oz of Greek Yoghurt

Protein 16g, Fat 40g, Carb 26g, Fibre 18g, 570 Kcals

Preparation

Place the nuts or seeds into the Tall Cup. Screw the Nutribullet Extractor Blade on to the top of the cup. Invert the cup, press it down into the Nutribullet Power Base and twist it into place. Blast them for 30 seconds. Put the rest of the solid ingredients into the cup and press them down below the Max Line. Add the fluid base to fill the cup up to the Max Line. Screw the Nutribullet Extractor Blade on to the top of the cup. Invert the cup, press it down into the Nutribullet Power Base and twist it into place. Blast the mixture until it is really smooth (20 or so seconds). ***Enjoy!***

Plum and Peach Paradise

Ingredients

1 Cup of Plum halves (120 grams or 4 oz)
1 Cup of Peach slices (120 grams or 4 oz)
30 grams or 1 oz of Peanuts
200 ml / 7 fl oz of Half Fat Crème Fraiche

Protein 10g, Fat 45g, Carb 35g, Fibre 6g, 610 Kcals

Preparation

Place the nuts or seeds into the Tall Cup. Screw the Nutribullet Extractor Blade on to the top of the cup. Invert the cup, press it down into the Nutribullet Power Base and twist it into place. Blast them for 30 seconds. Put the rest of the solid ingredients into the cup and press them down below the Max Line. Add the fluid base to fill the cup up to the Max Line. Screw the Nutribullet Extractor Blade on to the top of the cup. Invert the cup, press it down into the Nutribullet Power Base and twist it into place. Blast the mixture until it is really smooth (20 or so seconds). ***Enjoy!***

Prune Cleanser

Ingredients

2 Cups of Prunes (stoned) (240 grams or 8 oz)
30 grams or 1 oz of Brazil nuts
200 ml / 7 fl oz of Hazelnut Milk

Protein 7g, Fat 27g, Carb 15g, Fibre 9g, 265 Kcals

Preparation

Place the nuts or seeds into the Tall Cup. Screw the Nutribullet Extractor Blade on to the top of the cup. Invert the cup, press it down into the Nutribullet Power Base and twist it into place. Blast them for 30 seconds. Put the rest of the solid ingredients into the cup and press them down below the Max Line. Add the fluid base to fill the cup up to the Max Line. Screw the Nutribullet Extractor Blade on to the top of the cup. Invert the cup, press it down into the Nutribullet Power Base and twist it into place. Blast the mixture until it is really smooth (20 or so seconds). **Enjoy!**

Banana joins Pecan

Ingredients

1 Cup of Cranberries (120 grams or 4 oz)
1 small Banana (peeled and sliced) (120 grams or 4 oz)
30 grams or 1 oz of Pecans
200 ml / 7 fl oz of Coconut Milk

Protein 5g, Fat 24g, Carb 40g, Fibre 12g, 409 Kcals

Preparation

Place the nuts or seeds into the Tall Cup. Screw the Nutribullet Extractor Blade on to the top of the cup. Invert the cup, press it down into the Nutribullet Power Base and twist it into place. Blast them for 30 seconds. Put the rest of the solid ingredients into the cup and press them down below the Max Line. Add the fluid base to fill the cup up to the Max Line. Screw the Nutribullet Extractor Blade on to the top of the cup. Invert the cup, press it down into the Nutribullet Power Base and twist it into place. Blast the mixture until it is really smooth (20 or so seconds). **Enjoy!**

Peeled Fig and Hazelnut Feast

Ingredients

1 Cup of Peeled Figs (120 grams or 4 oz)
1 small Apple (cored) (120 grams or 4 oz)
30 grams or 1 oz of Hazelnuts
200 ml / 7 fl oz of Hazelnut Milk

Protein 6g, Fat 22g, Carb 41g, Fibre 10g, 397 Kcals

Preparation

Place the nuts or seeds into the Tall Cup. Screw the Nutribullet Extractor Blade on to the top of the cup. Invert the cup, press it down into the Nutribullet Power Base and twist it into place. Blast them for 30 seconds. Put the rest of the solid ingredients into the cup and press them down below the Max Line. Add the fluid base to fill the cup up to the Max Line. Screw the Nutribullet Extractor Blade on to the top of the cup. Invert the cup, press it down into the Nutribullet Power Base and twist it into place. Blast the mixture until it is really smooth (20 or so seconds). **Enjoy!**

Pear invites Almond

Ingredients

1 Cup of Blackberries (120 grams or 4 oz)
1 small Pear (cored) (120 grams or 4 oz)
30 grams or 1 oz of Almonds
200 ml / 7 fl oz of Greek Yoghurt

Protein 17g, Fat 36g, Carb 34g, Fibre 13g, 546 Kcals

Preparation

Place the nuts or seeds into the Tall Cup. Screw the Nutribullet Extractor Blade on to the top of the cup. Invert the cup, press it down into the Nutribullet Power Base and twist it into place. Blast them for 30 seconds. Put the rest of the solid ingredients into the cup and press them down below the Max Line. Add the fluid base to fill the cup up to the Max Line. Screw the Nutribullet Extractor Blade on to the top of the cup. Invert the cup, press it down into the Nutribullet Power Base and twist it into place. Blast the mixture until it is really smooth (20 or so seconds). **Enjoy!**

Strawberry Sunshine

Ingredients

1 Cup of Strawberries (120 grams or 4 oz)
1 Cup of Raspberries (120 grams or 4 oz)
30 grams or 1 oz of Cashews
200 ml / 7 fl oz of Coconut Milk

Protein 8g, Fat 16g, Carb 27g, Fibre 11g, 306 Kcals

Preparation

Place the nuts or seeds into the Tall Cup. Screw the Nutribullet Extractor Blade on to the top of the cup. Invert the cup, press it down into the Nutribullet Power Base and twist it into place. Blast them for 30 seconds. Put the rest of the solid ingredients into the cup and press them down below the Max Line. Add the fluid base to fill the cup up to the Max Line. Screw the Nutribullet Extractor Blade on to the top of the cup. Invert the cup, press it down into the Nutribullet Power Base and twist it into place. Blast the mixture until it is really smooth (20 or so seconds). **Enjoy!**

Date Dictator

Ingredients

2 Cups of Dates (stoned) (240 grams or 8 oz)
30 grams or 1 oz of Almonds
200 ml / 7 fl oz of Half Fat Crème Fraiche

Protein 12g, Fat 47g, Carb 174g, Fibre 22g, 1191 Kcals

Preparation

Place the nuts or seeds into the Tall Cup. Screw the Nutribullet Extractor Blade on to the top of the cup. Invert the cup, press it down into the Nutribullet Power Base and twist it into place. Blast them for 30 seconds. Put the rest of the solid ingredients into the cup and press them down below the Max Line. Add the fluid base to fill the cup up to the Max Line. Screw the Nutribullet Extractor Blade on to the top of the cup. Invert the cup, press it down into the Nutribullet Power Base and twist it into place. Blast the mixture until it is really smooth (20 or so seconds). **Enjoy!**

Prune meets Peanut

Ingredients

1 Cup of Prunes (stoned) (120 grams or 4 oz)
1 Cup of Red Grapes (120 grams or 4 oz)
30 grams or 1 oz of Peanuts
200 ml / 7 fl oz of Greek Yoghurt

Protein 18g, Fat 36g, Carb 38g, Fibre 7g, 507 Kcals

Preparation

Place the nuts or seeds into the Tall Cup. Screw the Nutribullet Extractor Blade on to the top of the cup. Invert the cup, press it down into the Nutribullet Power Base and twist it into place. Blast them for 30 seconds. Put the rest of the solid ingredients into the cup and press them down below the Max Line. Add the fluid base to fill the cup up to the Max Line. Screw the Nutribullet Extractor Blade on to the top of the cup. Invert the cup, press it down into the Nutribullet Power Base and twist it into place. Blast the mixture until it is really smooth (20 or so seconds). **Enjoy!**

Blueberry and Goji Heaven

Ingredients

1 Cup of Blueberries (120 grams or 4 oz)
½ Cup of Goji Berries Dried (40 grams or 1½ oz)
30 grams or 1 oz of Walnuts
200 ml / 7 fl oz of Half Fat Crème Fraiche

Protein 11g, Fat 51g, Carb 50g, Fibre 7g, 730 Kcals

Preparation

Place the nuts or seeds into the Tall Cup. Screw the Nutribullet Extractor Blade on to the top of the cup. Invert the cup, press it down into the Nutribullet Power Base and twist it into place. Blast them for 30 seconds. Put the rest of the solid ingredients into the cup and press them down below the Max Line. Add the fluid base to fill the cup up to the Max Line. Screw the Nutribullet Extractor Blade on to the top of the cup. Invert the cup, press it down into the Nutribullet Power Base and twist it into place. Blast the mixture until it is really smooth (20 or so seconds). **Enjoy!**

Guava on Clementine

Ingredients

1 Cup of Guava (120 grams or 4 oz)
1 Cup of Clementine slices (120 grams or 4 oz)
30 grams or 1 oz of Hazelnuts
200 ml / 7 fl oz of Hazelnut Milk

Protein 9g, Fat 23g, Carb 31g, Fibre 12g, 384 Kcals

Preparation

Place the nuts or seeds into the Tall Cup. Screw the Nutribullet Extractor Blade on to the top of the cup. Invert the cup, press it down into the Nutribullet Power Base and twist it into place. Blast them for 30 seconds. Put the rest of the solid ingredients into the cup and press them down below the Max Line. Add the fluid base to fill the cup up to the Max Line. Screw the Nutribullet Extractor Blade on to the top of the cup. Invert the cup, press it down into the Nutribullet Power Base and twist it into place. Blast the mixture until it is really smooth (20 or so seconds). **Enjoy!**

Melon and Cashew Delivered

Ingredients

1 Cup of Melon chunks (120 grams or 4 oz)
1 Cup of Nectarine segments (120 grams or 4 oz)
30 grams or 1 oz of Cashews
200 ml / 7 fl oz of Coconut Milk

Protein 8g, Fat 16g, Carb 34g, Fibre 4g, 301 Kcals

Preparation

Place the nuts or seeds into the Tall Cup. Screw the Nutribullet Extractor Blade on to the top of the cup. Invert the cup, press it down into the Nutribullet Power Base and twist it into place. Blast them for 30 seconds. Put the rest of the solid ingredients into the cup and press them down below the Max Line. Add the fluid base to fill the cup up to the Max Line. Screw the Nutribullet Extractor Blade on to the top of the cup. Invert the cup, press it down into the Nutribullet Power Base and twist it into place. Blast the mixture until it is really smooth (20 or so seconds). **Enjoy!**

Orange Orchard

Ingredients

1 Cup of Orange segments (120 grams or 4 oz)
1 Cup of Cherries (stoned) (120 grams or 4 oz)
30 grams or 1 oz of Pecans
200 ml / 7 fl oz of Coconut Milk

Protein 5g, Fat 24g, Carb 35g, Fibre 8g, 379 Kcals

Preparation

Place the nuts or seeds into the Tall Cup. Screw the Nutribullet Extractor Blade on to the top of the cup. Invert the cup, press it down into the Nutribullet Power Base and twist it into place. Blast them for 30 seconds. Put the rest of the solid ingredients into the cup and press them down below the Max Line. Add the fluid base to fill the cup up to the Max Line. Screw the Nutribullet Extractor Blade on to the top of the cup. Invert the cup, press it down into the Nutribullet Power Base and twist it into place. Blast the mixture until it is really smooth (20 or so seconds). **Enjoy!**

Kiwi embraces Brazil

Ingredients

2 Cups of Kiwi Fruit slices (240 grams or 8 oz)
30 grams or 1 oz of Brazil nuts
200 ml / 7 fl oz of Half Fat Crème Fraiche

Protein 7g, Fat 51g, Carb 40g, Fibre 9g, 682 Kcals

Preparation

Place the nuts or seeds into the Tall Cup. Screw the Nutribullet Extractor Blade on to the top of the cup. Invert the cup, press it down into the Nutribullet Power Base and twist it into place. Blast them for 30 seconds. Put the rest of the solid ingredients into the cup and press them down below the Max Line. Add the fluid base to fill the cup up to the Max Line. Screw the Nutribullet Extractor Blade on to the top of the cup. Invert the cup, press it down into the Nutribullet Power Base and twist it into place. Blast the mixture until it is really smooth (20 or so seconds). **Enjoy!**

Tangerine and Pineapple Piazza

Ingredients

1 Cup of Tangerine slices (120 grams or 4 oz)
1 Cup of Pineapple chunks (120 grams or 4 oz)
30 grams or 1 oz of Pecans
200 ml / 7 fl oz of Hazelnut Milk

Protein 5g, Fat 25g, Carb 35g, Fibre 7g, 388 Kcals

Preparation

Place the nuts or seeds into the Tall Cup. Screw the Nutribullet Extractor Blade on to the top of the cup. Invert the cup, press it down into the Nutribullet Power Base and twist it into place. Blast them for 30 seconds. Put the rest of the solid ingredients into the cup and press them down below the Max Line. Add the fluid base to fill the cup up to the Max Line. Screw the Nutribullet Extractor Blade on to the top of the cup. Invert the cup, press it down into the Nutribullet Power Base and twist it into place. Blast the mixture until it is really smooth (20 or so seconds). **Enjoy!**

Tangerine and Peanut Nexus

Ingredients

2 Cups of Tangerine slices (240 grams or 8 oz)
30 grams or 1 oz of Peanuts
200 ml / 7 fl oz of Greek Yoghurt

Protein 18g, Fat 35g, Carb 41g, Fibre 7g, 547 Kcals

Preparation

Place the nuts or seeds into the Tall Cup. Screw the Nutribullet Extractor Blade on to the top of the cup. Invert the cup, press it down into the Nutribullet Power Base and twist it into place. Blast them for 30 seconds. Put the rest of the solid ingredients into the cup and press them down below the Max Line. Add the fluid base to fill the cup up to the Max Line. Screw the Nutribullet Extractor Blade on to the top of the cup. Invert the cup, press it down into the Nutribullet Power Base and twist it into place. Blast the mixture until it is really smooth (20 or so seconds). **Enjoy!**

Kiwi goes Walnut

Ingredients

1 Cup of Water Melon chunks (120 grams or 4 oz)
1 Cup of Kiwi Fruit slices (120 grams or 4 oz)
30 grams or 1 oz of Walnuts
200 ml / 7 fl oz of Hazelnut Milk

Protein 7g, Fat 24g, Carb 31g, Fibre 7g, 363 Kcals

Preparation

Place the nuts or seeds into the Tall Cup. Screw the Nutribullet Extractor Blade on to the top of the cup. Invert the cup, press it down into the Nutribullet Power Base and twist it into place. Blast them for 30 seconds. Put the rest of the solid ingredients into the cup and press them down below the Max Line. Add the fluid base to fill the cup up to the Max Line. Screw the Nutribullet Extractor Blade on to the top of the cup. Invert the cup, press it down into the Nutribullet Power Base and twist it into place. Blast the mixture until it is really smooth (20 or so seconds). **Enjoy!**

Papaya and Almond Seduction

Ingredients

1 Cup of Grapefruit segments (120 grams or 4 oz)
1 Cup of Papaya (120 grams or 4 oz)
30 grams or 1 oz of Almonds
200 ml / 7 fl oz of Coconut Milk

Protein 8g, Fat 18g, Carb 27g, Fibre 6g, 307 Kcals

Preparation

Place the nuts or seeds into the Tall Cup. Screw the Nutribullet Extractor Blade on to the top of the cup. Invert the cup, press it down into the Nutribullet Power Base and twist it into place. Blast them for 30 seconds. Put the rest of the solid ingredients into the cup and press them down below the Max Line. Add the fluid base to fill the cup up to the Max Line. Screw the Nutribullet Extractor Blade on to the top of the cup. Invert the cup, press it down into the Nutribullet Power Base and twist it into place. Blast the mixture until it is really smooth (20 or so seconds). **Enjoy!**

Cashew Chorus

Ingredients

1 Cup of Dates (stoned) (120 grams or 4 oz)
1 Cup of Mango slices (120 grams or 4 oz)
30 grams or 1 oz of Cashews
200 ml / 7 fl oz of Half Fat Crème Fraiche

Protein 10g, Fat 44g, Carb 116g, Fibre 13g, 914 Kcals

Preparation

Place the nuts or seeds into the Tall Cup. Screw the Nutribullet Extractor Blade on to the top of the cup. Invert the cup, press it down into the Nutribullet Power Base and twist it into place. Blast them for 30 seconds. Put the rest of the solid ingredients into the cup and press them down below the Max Line. Add the fluid base to fill the cup up to the Max Line. Screw the Nutribullet Extractor Blade on to the top of the cup. Invert the cup, press it down into the Nutribullet Power Base and twist it into place. Blast the mixture until it is really smooth (20 or so seconds). **Enjoy!**

Mango joins Goji

Ingredients

1 Cup of Mango slices (120 grams or 4 oz)
½ Cup of Goji Berries Dried (40 grams or 1½ oz)
30 grams or 1 oz of Hazelnuts
200 ml / 7 fl oz of Greek Yoghurt

Protein 19g, Fat 38g, Carb 52g, Fibre 7g, 638 Kcals

Preparation

Place the nuts or seeds into the Tall Cup. Screw the Nutribullet Extractor Blade on to the top of the cup. Invert the cup, press it down into the Nutribullet Power Base and twist it into place. Blast them for 30 seconds. Put the rest of the solid ingredients into the cup and press them down below the Max Line. Add the fluid base to fill the cup up to the Max Line. Screw the Nutribullet Extractor Blade on to the top of the cup. Invert the cup, press it down into the Nutribullet Power Base and twist it into place. Blast the mixture until it is really smooth (20 or so seconds). **Enjoy!**

Fennel Fiesta

Ingredients

1 Cup/Handful of Fennel (40 grams or 1½ oz)
1 Cup/Handful of Broccoli Florets (40 grams or 1½ oz)
1 Cup of Blackberries (120 grams or 4 oz)
1 Cup of Grapefruit segments (120 grams or 4 oz)
22 grams or ¾ oz of Chia Seeds
200 ml / 7 fl oz of Almond Milk (Unsweetened)

Protein 8g, Fat 10g, Carb 19g, Fibre 18g, 248 Kcals

Preparation

Place the nuts or seeds into the Tall Cup. Screw the Nutribullet Extractor Blade on to the top of the cup. Invert the cup, press it down into the Nutribullet Power Base and twist it into place. Blast them for 30 seconds. Put the rest of the solid ingredients into the cup and press them down below the Max Line. Add the fluid base to fill the cup up to the Max Line. Screw the Nutribullet Extractor Blade on to the top of the cup. Invert the cup, press it down into the Nutribullet Power Base and twist it into place. Blast the mixture until it is really smooth (20 or so seconds). **Enjoy!**

Walnut Waterfall

Ingredients

1 Cup/Handful of Lettuce Leaves (40 grams or 1½ oz)
1 Cup/Handful of Rocket/Arugura Lettuce (40 grams or 1½ oz)
1 small Apple (cored) (120 grams or 4 oz)
1 Cup of Nectarine segments (120 grams or 4 oz)
30 grams or 1 oz of Walnuts
200 ml / 7 fl oz of Dairy Milk Whole

Protein 14g, Fat 28g, Carb 37g, Fibre 8g, 452 Kcals

Preparation

Place the nuts or seeds into the Tall Cup. Screw the Nutribullet Extractor Blade on to the top of the cup. Invert the cup, press it down into the Nutribullet Power Base and twist it into place. Blast them for 30 seconds. Put the rest of the solid ingredients into the cup and press them down below the Max Line. Add the fluid base to fill the cup up to the Max Line. Screw the Nutribullet Extractor Blade on to the top of the cup. Invert the cup, press it down into the Nutribullet Power Base and twist it into place. Blast the mixture until it is really smooth (20 or so seconds). **Enjoy!**

Red Cabbage Cascade

Ingredients

1 Cup/Handful of Bok Choy (40 grams or 1½ oz)
1 Cup/Handful of Red or White Cabbage (40 grams or 1½ oz)
1 Cup of Plum halves (120 grams or 4 oz)
1 small Avocado (stoned and peeled) (120 grams or 4 oz)
30 grams or 1 oz of Almonds
200 ml / 7 fl oz of Coconut Milk

Protein 11g, Fat 36g, Carb 24g, Fibre 14g, 481 Kcals

Preparation

Place the nuts or seeds into the Tall Cup. Screw the Nutribullet Extractor Blade on to the top of the cup. Invert the cup, press it down into the Nutribullet Power Base and twist it into place. Blast them for 30 seconds. Put the rest of the solid ingredients into the cup and press them down below the Max Line. Add the fluid base to fill the cup up to the Max Line. Screw the Nutribullet Extractor Blade on to the top of the cup. Invert the cup, press it down into the Nutribullet Power Base and twist it into place. Blast the mixture until it is really smooth (20 or so seconds). **Enjoy!**

Water Melon Miracle

Ingredients

2 Cups/Handfuls of Red or White Cabbage (80 grams or 3 oz)
1 Cup of Strawberries (120 grams or 4 oz)
1 Cup of Water Melon chunks (120 grams or 4 oz)
22 grams or ¾ oz of Flax Seeds
200 ml / 7 fl oz of Water

Protein 7g, Fat 10g, Carb 20g, Fibre 11g, 216 Kcals

Preparation

Place the nuts or seeds into the Tall Cup. Screw the Nutribullet Extractor Blade on to the top of the cup. Invert the cup, press it down into the Nutribullet Power Base and twist it into place. Blast them for 30 seconds. Put the rest of the solid ingredients into the cup and press them down below the Max Line. Add the fluid base to fill the cup up to the Max Line. Screw the Nutribullet Extractor Blade on to the top of the cup. Invert the cup, press it down into the Nutribullet Power Base and twist it into place. Blast the mixture until it is really smooth (20 or so seconds). **Enjoy!**

Tangerine goes Raspberry

Ingredients

2 Cups/Handfuls of Watercress (80 grams or 3 oz)
1 Cup of Tangerine slices (120 grams or 4 oz)
1 Cup of Raspberries (120 grams or 4 oz)
30 grams or 1 oz of Cashews
200 ml / 7 fl oz of Hazelnut Milk

Protein 10g, Fat 18g, Carb 35g, Fibre 12g, 358 Kcals

Preparation

Place the nuts or seeds into the Tall Cup. Screw the Nutribullet Extractor Blade on to the top of the cup. Invert the cup, press it down into the Nutribullet Power Base and twist it into place. Blast them for 30 seconds. Put the rest of the solid ingredients into the cup and press them down below the Max Line. Add the fluid base to fill the cup up to the Max Line. Screw the Nutribullet Extractor Blade on to the top of the cup. Invert the cup, press it down into the Nutribullet Power Base and twist it into place. Blast the mixture until it is really smooth (20 or so seconds). **Enjoy!**

Green Cabbage meets Mango

Ingredients

1 Cup/Handful of Green Cabbage (40 grams or 1½ oz)
1 Cup/Handful of Spinach (40 grams or 1½ oz)
1 small Pear (cored) (120 grams or 4 oz)
1 Cup of Mango slices (120 grams or 4 oz)
22 grams or ¾ oz of Pumpkin Seeds
200 ml / 7 fl oz of Half Fat Crème Fraiche

Protein 9g, Fat 40g, Carb 47g, Fibre 9g, 621 Kcals

Preparation

Place the nuts or seeds into the Tall Cup. Screw the Nutribullet Extractor Blade on to the top of the cup. Invert the cup, press it down into the Nutribullet Power Base and twist it into place. Blast them for 30 seconds. Put the rest of the solid ingredients into the cup and press them down below the Max Line. Add the fluid base to fill the cup up to the Max Line. Screw the Nutribullet Extractor Blade on to the top of the cup. Invert the cup, press it down into the Nutribullet Power Base and twist it into place. Blast the mixture until it is really smooth (20 or so seconds). **Enjoy!**

Melon Melody

Ingredients

1 Cup/Handful of Mint (40 grams or 1½ oz)
1 Cup/Handful of Watercress (40 grams or 1½ oz)
1 Cup of Clementine slices (120 grams or 4 oz)
1 Cup of Melon chunks (120 grams or 4 oz)
30 grams or 1 oz of Pecans
200 ml / 7 fl oz of Greek Yoghurt

Protein 15g, Fat 41g, Carb 36g, Fibre 9g, 578 Kcals

Preparation

Place the nuts or seeds into the Tall Cup. Screw the Nutribullet Extractor Blade on to the top of the cup. Invert the cup, press it down into the Nutribullet Power Base and twist it into place. Blast them for 30 seconds. Put the rest of the solid ingredients into the cup and press them down below the Max Line. Add the fluid base to fill the cup up to the Max Line. Screw the Nutribullet Extractor Blade on to the top of the cup. Invert the cup, press it down into the Nutribullet Power Base and twist it into place. Blast the mixture until it is really smooth (20 or so seconds). **Enjoy!**

Watercress and Brazil Royale

Ingredients

1 Cup/Handful of Watercress (40 grams or 1½ oz)
1 Cup/Handful of Mint (40 grams or 1½ oz)
2 Cups of Mango slices (240 grams or 8 oz)
30 grams or 1 oz of Brazil nuts
200 ml / 7 fl oz of Greek Yoghurt

Protein 17g, Fat 40g, Carb 45g, Fibre 9g, 613 Kcals

Preparation

Place the nuts or seeds into the Tall Cup. Screw the Nutribullet Extractor Blade on to the top of the cup. Invert the cup, press it down into the Nutribullet Power Base and twist it into place. Blast them for 30 seconds. Put the rest of the solid ingredients into the cup and press them down below the Max Line. Add the fluid base to fill the cup up to the Max Line. Screw the Nutribullet Extractor Blade on to the top of the cup. Invert the cup, press it down into the Nutribullet Power Base and twist it into place. Blast the mixture until it is really smooth (20 or so seconds). **Enjoy!**

Green Cabbage Crush

Ingredients

1 Cup/Handful of Green Cabbage (40 grams or 1½ oz)
1 Cup/Handful of Broccoli Florets (40 grams or 1½ oz)
1 Cup of Kiwi Fruit slices (120 grams or 4 oz)
1 Cup of Peeled Figs (120 grams or 4 oz)
30 grams or 1 oz of Peanuts
200 ml / 7 fl oz of Almond Milk (Unsweetened)

Protein 12g, Fat 18g, Carb 39g, Fibre 12g, 381 Kcals

Preparation

Place the nuts or seeds into the Tall Cup. Screw the Nutribullet Extractor Blade on to the top of the cup. Invert the cup, press it down into the Nutribullet Power Base and twist it into place. Blast them for 30 seconds. Put the rest of the solid ingredients into the cup and press them down below the Max Line. Add the fluid base to fill the cup up to the Max Line. Screw the Nutribullet Extractor Blade on to the top of the cup. Invert the cup, press it down into the Nutribullet Power Base and twist it into place. Blast the mixture until it is really smooth (20 or so seconds). **Enjoy!**

Rocket and Blueberry Feast

Ingredients

1 Cup/Handful of Rocket/Arugura Lettuce (40 grams or 1½ oz)
1 Cup/Handful of Fennel (40 grams or 1½ oz)
1 Cup of Cherries (stoned) (120 grams or 4 oz)
1 Cup of Blueberries (120 grams or 4 oz)
30 grams or 1 oz of Hazelnuts
200 ml / 7 fl oz of Water

Protein 8g, Fat 19g, Carb 36g, Fibre 10g, 350 Kcals

Preparation

Place the nuts or seeds into the Tall Cup. Screw the Nutribullet Extractor Blade on to the top of the cup. Invert the cup, press it down into the Nutribullet Power Base and twist it into place. Blast them for 30 seconds. Put the rest of the solid ingredients into the cup and press them down below the Max Line. Add the fluid base to fill the cup up to the Max Line. Screw the Nutribullet Extractor Blade on to the top of the cup. Invert the cup, press it down into the Nutribullet Power Base and twist it into place. Blast the mixture until it is really smooth (20 or so seconds). **Enjoy!**

Broccoli embraces Peach

Ingredients

2 Cups/Handfuls of Broccoli Florets (80 grams or 3 oz)
1 Cup of Pineapple chunks (120 grams or 4 oz)
1 Cup of Peach slices (120 grams or 4 oz)
22 grams or ¾ oz of Sunflower Seeds Hulled
200 ml / 7 fl oz of Hazelnut Milk

Protein 9g, Fat 14g, Carb 36g, Fibre 7g, 305 Kcals

Preparation

Place the nuts or seeds into the Tall Cup. Screw the Nutribullet Extractor Blade on to the top of the cup. Invert the cup, press it down into the Nutribullet Power Base and twist it into place. Blast them for 30 seconds. Put the rest of the solid ingredients into the cup and press them down below the Max Line. Add the fluid base to fill the cup up to the Max Line. Screw the Nutribullet Extractor Blade on to the top of the cup. Invert the cup, press it down into the Nutribullet Power Base and twist it into place. Blast the mixture until it is really smooth (20 or so seconds). **Enjoy!**

Banana loves Sesame

Ingredients

1 Cup/Handful of Lettuce Leaves (40 grams or 1½ oz)
1 Cup/Handful of Red or White Cabbage (40 grams or 1½ oz)
1 small Banana (peeled and sliced) (120 grams or 4 oz)
1 Cup of Guava (120 grams or 4 oz)
22 grams or ¾ oz of Sesame Seeds Hulled
200 ml / 7 fl oz of Coconut Milk

Protein 10g, Fat 16g, Carb 43g, Fibre 13g, 379 Kcals

Preparation

Place the nuts or seeds into the Tall Cup. Screw the Nutribullet Extractor Blade on to the top of the cup. Invert the cup, press it down into the Nutribullet Power Base and twist it into place. Blast them for 30 seconds. Put the rest of the solid ingredients into the cup and press them down below the Max Line. Add the fluid base to fill the cup up to the Max Line. Screw the Nutribullet Extractor Blade on to the top of the cup. Invert the cup, press it down into the Nutribullet Power Base and twist it into place. Blast the mixture until it is really smooth (20 or so seconds). **Enjoy!**

Red Grape in Apricot

Ingredients

1 Cup/Handful of Spinach (40 grams or 1½ oz)
1 Cup/Handful of Bok Choy (40 grams or 1½ oz)
1 Cup of Red Grapes (120 grams or 4 oz)
1 Cup of Apricot halves (120 grams or 4 oz)
22 grams or ¾ oz of Sunflower Seeds Hulled
200 ml / 7 fl oz of Dairy Milk Whole

Protein 15g, Fat 19g, Carb 45g, Fibre 6g, 396 Kcals

Preparation

Place the nuts or seeds into the Tall Cup. Screw the Nutribullet Extractor Blade on to the top of the cup. Invert the cup, press it down into the Nutribullet Power Base and twist it into place. Blast them for 30 seconds. Put the rest of the solid ingredients into the cup and press them down below the Max Line. Add the fluid base to fill the cup up to the Max Line. Screw the Nutribullet Extractor Blade on to the top of the cup. Invert the cup, press it down into the Nutribullet Power Base and twist it into place. Blast the mixture until it is really smooth (20 or so seconds). **Enjoy!**

Lettuce Lagoon

Ingredients

1 Cup/Handful of Fennel (40 grams or 1½ oz)
1 Cup/Handful of Lettuce Leaves (40 grams or 1½ oz)
2 Cups of Cranberries (240 grams or 8 oz)
30 grams or 1 oz of Brazil nuts
200 ml / 7 fl oz of Half Fat Crème Fraiche

Protein 6g, Fat 51g, Carb 33g, Fibre 15g, 665 Kcals

Preparation

Place the nuts or seeds into the Tall Cup. Screw the Nutribullet Extractor Blade on to the top of the cup. Invert the cup, press it down into the Nutribullet Power Base and twist it into place. Blast them for 30 seconds. Put the rest of the solid ingredients into the cup and press them down below the Max Line. Add the fluid base to fill the cup up to the Max Line. Screw the Nutribullet Extractor Blade on to the top of the cup. Invert the cup, press it down into the Nutribullet Power Base and twist it into place. Blast the mixture until it is really smooth (20 or so seconds). **Enjoy!**

Watercress and Orange Revelation
Ingredients

2 Cups/Handfuls of Watercress (80 grams or 3 oz)
1 Cup of Orange segments (120 grams or 4 oz)
1 Cup of Prunes (stoned) (120 grams or 4 oz)
30 grams or 1 oz of Almonds
200 ml / 7 fl oz of Almond Milk (Unsweetened)

Protein 11g, Fat 20g, Carb 18g, Fibre 10g, 273 Kcals

Preparation

Place the nuts or seeds into the Tall Cup. Screw the Nutribullet Extractor Blade on to the top of the cup. Invert the cup, press it down into the Nutribullet Power Base and twist it into place. Blast them for 30 seconds. Put the rest of the solid ingredients into the cup and press them down below the Max Line. Add the fluid base to fill the cup up to the Max Line. Screw the Nutribullet Extractor Blade on to the top of the cup. Invert the cup, press it down into the Nutribullet Power Base and twist it into place. Blast the mixture until it is really smooth (20 or so seconds). **Enjoy!**

Goji Guru
Ingredients

2 Cups/Handfuls of Bok Choy (80 grams or 3 oz)
1 Cup of Papaya (120 grams or 4 oz)
½ Cup of Goji Berries Dried (40 grams or 1½ oz)
30 grams or 1 oz of Cashews
200 ml / 7 fl oz of Water

Protein 13g, Fat 14g, Carb 43g, Fibre 6g, 356 Kcals

Preparation

Place the nuts or seeds into the Tall Cup. Screw the Nutribullet Extractor Blade on to the top of the cup. Invert the cup, press it down into the Nutribullet Power Base and twist it into place. Blast them for 30 seconds. Put the rest of the solid ingredients into the cup and press them down below the Max Line. Add the fluid base to fill the cup up to the Max Line. Screw the Nutribullet Extractor Blade on to the top of the cup. Invert the cup, press it down into the Nutribullet Power Base and twist it into place. Blast the mixture until it is really smooth (20 or so seconds). **Enjoy!**

Cranberry Holiday

Ingredients

1 Cup/Handful of Watercress (40 grams or 1½ oz)
1 Cup/Handful of Red or White Cabbage (40 grams or 1½ oz)
1 Cup of Cranberries (120 grams or 4 oz)
1 Cup of Dates (stoned) (120 grams or 4 oz)
30 grams or 1 oz of Walnuts
200 ml / 7 fl oz of Dairy Milk Whole

Protein 16g, Fat 27g, Carb 103g, Fibre 18g, 734 Kcals

Preparation

Place the nuts or seeds into the Tall Cup. Screw the Nutribullet Extractor Blade on to the top of the cup. Invert the cup, press it down into the Nutribullet Power Base and twist it into place. Blast them for 30 seconds. Put the rest of the solid ingredients into the cup and press them down below the Max Line. Add the fluid base to fill the cup up to the Max Line. Screw the Nutribullet Extractor Blade on to the top of the cup. Invert the cup, press it down into the Nutribullet Power Base and twist it into place. Blast the mixture until it is really smooth (20 or so seconds). **Enjoy!**

Kiwi finds Sesame

Ingredients

1 Cup/Handful of Bok Choy (40 grams or 1½ oz)
1 Cup/Handful of Spinach (40 grams or 1½ oz)
2 Cups of Kiwi Fruit slices (240 grams or 8 oz)
22 grams or ¾ oz of Sesame Seeds Hulled
200 ml / 7 fl oz of Half Fat Crème Fraiche

Protein 9g, Fat 44g, Carb 40g, Fibre 10g, 630 Kcals

Preparation

Place the nuts or seeds into the Tall Cup. Screw the Nutribullet Extractor Blade on to the top of the cup. Invert the cup, press it down into the Nutribullet Power Base and twist it into place. Blast them for 30 seconds. Put the rest of the solid ingredients into the cup and press them down below the Max Line. Add the fluid base to fill the cup up to the Max Line. Screw the Nutribullet Extractor Blade on to the top of the cup. Invert the cup, press it down into the Nutribullet Power Base and twist it into place. Blast the mixture until it is really smooth (20 or so seconds). **Enjoy!**

Green Cabbage joins Peeled Fig

Ingredients

1 Cup/Handful of Broccoli Florets (40 grams or 1½ oz)
1 Cup/Handful of Green Cabbage (40 grams or 1½ oz)
1 Cup of Peeled Figs (120 grams or 4 oz)
1 Cup of Cherries (stoned) (120 grams or 4 oz)
30 grams or 1 oz of Peanuts
200 ml / 7 fl oz of Hazelnut Milk

Protein 12g, Fat 19g, Carb 47g, Fibre 11g, 416 Kcals

Preparation

Place the nuts or seeds into the Tall Cup. Screw the Nutribullet Extractor Blade on to the top of the cup. Invert the cup, press it down into the Nutribullet Power Base and twist it into place. Blast them for 30 seconds. Put the rest of the solid ingredients into the cup and press them down below the Max Line. Add the fluid base to fill the cup up to the Max Line. Screw the Nutribullet Extractor Blade on to the top of the cup. Invert the cup, press it down into the Nutribullet Power Base and twist it into place. Blast the mixture until it is really smooth (20 or so seconds). **Enjoy!**

Grapefruit needs Pecan

Ingredients

1 Cup/Handful of Rocket/Arugura Lettuce (40 grams or 1½ oz)
1 Cup/Handful of Mint (40 grams or 1½ oz)
1 Cup of Grapefruit segments (120 grams or 4 oz)
1 Cup of Mango slices (120 grams or 4 oz)
30 grams or 1 oz of Pecans
200 ml / 7 fl oz of Greek Yoghurt

Protein 15g, Fat 42g, Carb 38g, Fibre 9g, 591 Kcals

Preparation

Place the nuts or seeds into the Tall Cup. Screw the Nutribullet Extractor Blade on to the top of the cup. Invert the cup, press it down into the Nutribullet Power Base and twist it into place. Blast them for 30 seconds. Put the rest of the solid ingredients into the cup and press them down below the Max Line. Add the fluid base to fill the cup up to the Max Line. Screw the Nutribullet Extractor Blade on to the top of the cup. Invert the cup, press it down into the Nutribullet Power Base and twist it into place. Blast the mixture until it is really smooth (20 or so seconds). **Enjoy!**

Nectarine on Apple

Ingredients

1 Cup/Handful of Watercress (40 grams or 1½ oz)
1 Cup/Handful of Bok Choy (40 grams or 1½ oz)
1 Cup of Nectarine segments (120 grams or 4 oz)
1 small Apple (cored) (120 grams or 4 oz)
22 grams or ¾ oz of Pumpkin Seeds
200 ml / 7 fl oz of Coconut Milk

Protein 9g, Fat 12g, Carb 33g, Fibre 7g, 289 Kcals

Preparation

Place the nuts or seeds into the Tall Cup. Screw the Nutribullet Extractor Blade on to the top of the cup. Invert the cup, press it down into the Nutribullet Power Base and twist it into place. Blast them for 30 seconds. Put the rest of the solid ingredients into the cup and press them down below the Max Line. Add the fluid base to fill the cup up to the Max Line. Screw the Nutribullet Extractor Blade on to the top of the cup. Invert the cup, press it down into the Nutribullet Power Base and twist it into place. Blast the mixture until it is really smooth (20 or so seconds). **Enjoy!**

Rocket and Blackberry Vortex

Ingredients

1 Cup/Handful of Rocket/Arugura Lettuce (40 grams or 1½ oz)
1 Cup/Handful of Broccoli Florets (40 grams or 1½ oz)
1 Cup of Dates (stoned) (120 grams or 4 oz)
1 Cup of Blackberries (120 grams or 4 oz)
22 grams or ¾ oz of Chia Seeds
200 ml / 7 fl oz of Hazelnut Milk

Protein 11g, Fat 11g, Carb 96g, Fibre 26g, 574 Kcals

Preparation

Place the nuts or seeds into the Tall Cup. Screw the Nutribullet Extractor Blade on to the top of the cup. Invert the cup, press it down into the Nutribullet Power Base and twist it into place. Blast them for 30 seconds. Put the rest of the solid ingredients into the cup and press them down below the Max Line. Add the fluid base to fill the cup up to the Max Line. Screw the Nutribullet Extractor Blade on to the top of the cup. Invert the cup, press it down into the Nutribullet Power Base and twist it into place. Blast the mixture until it is really smooth (20 or so seconds). **Enjoy!**

Rocket Regatta

Ingredients

2 Cups/Handfuls of Rocket/Arugura Lettuce (80 grams or 3 oz)
1 Cup of Pineapple chunks (120 grams or 4 oz)
1 small Pear (cored) (120 grams or 4 oz)
22 grams or ¾ oz of Flax Seeds
200 ml / 7 fl oz of Dairy Milk Whole

Protein 13g, Fat 17g, Carb 41g, Fibre 12g, 385 Kcals

Preparation

Place the nuts or seeds into the Tall Cup. Screw the Nutribullet Extractor Blade on to the top of the cup. Invert the cup, press it down into the Nutribullet Power Base and twist it into place. Blast them for 30 seconds. Put the rest of the solid ingredients into the cup and press them down below the Max Line. Add the fluid base to fill the cup up to the Max Line. Screw the Nutribullet Extractor Blade on to the top of the cup. Invert the cup, press it down into the Nutribullet Power Base and twist it into place. Blast the mixture until it is really smooth (20 or so seconds). **Enjoy!**

Guava and Hazelnut Detente

Ingredients

1 Cup/Handful of Spinach (40 grams or 1½ oz)
1 Cup/Handful of Lettuce Leaves (40 grams or 1½ oz)
1 Cup of Cranberries (120 grams or 4 oz)
1 Cup of Guava (120 grams or 4 oz)
30 grams or 1 oz of Hazelnuts
200 ml / 7 fl oz of Water

Protein 10g, Fat 20g, Carb 23g, Fibre 17g, 341 Kcals

Preparation

Place the nuts or seeds into the Tall Cup. Screw the Nutribullet Extractor Blade on to the top of the cup. Invert the cup, press it down into the Nutribullet Power Base and twist it into place. Blast them for 30 seconds. Put the rest of the solid ingredients into the cup and press them down below the Max Line. Add the fluid base to fill the cup up to the Max Line. Screw the Nutribullet Extractor Blade on to the top of the cup. Invert the cup, press it down into the Nutribullet Power Base and twist it into place. Blast the mixture until it is really smooth (20 or so seconds). **Enjoy!**

Peach Paradox

Ingredients

1 Cup/Handful of Green Cabbage (40 grams or 1½ oz)
1 Cup/Handful of Red or White Cabbage (40 grams or 1½ oz)
1 Cup of Peach slices (120 grams or 4 oz)
1 Cup of Water Melon chunks (120 grams or 4 oz)
30 grams or 1 oz of Walnuts
200 ml / 7 fl oz of Almond Milk (Unsweetened)

Protein 8g, Fat 22g, Carb 24g, Fibre 7g, 327 Kcals

Preparation

Place the nuts or seeds into the Tall Cup. Screw the Nutribullet Extractor Blade on to the top of the cup. Invert the cup, press it down into the Nutribullet Power Base and twist it into place. Blast them for 30 seconds. Put the rest of the solid ingredients into the cup and press them down below the Max Line. Add the fluid base to fill the cup up to the Max Line. Screw the Nutribullet Extractor Blade on to the top of the cup. Invert the cup, press it down into the Nutribullet Power Base and twist it into place. Blast the mixture until it is really smooth (20 or so seconds). **Enjoy!**

Celeriac Cascade

Ingredients

1 Cup/Handful of Spinach (40 grams or 1½ oz)
1 Cup/Handful of Watercress (40 grams or 1½ oz)
1 Cup of Plum halves (120 grams or 4 oz)
1 Cup of diced Celeriac (120 grams or 4 oz)
22 grams or ¾ oz of Chia Seeds
200 ml / 7 fl oz of Greek Yoghurt

Protein 17g, Fat 27g, Carb 34g, Fibre 12g, 476 Kcals

Preparation

Place the nuts or seeds into the Tall Cup. Screw the Nutribullet Extractor Blade on to the top of the cup. Invert the cup, press it down into the Nutribullet Power Base and twist it into place. Blast them for 30 seconds. Put the rest of the solid ingredients into the cup and press them down below the Max Line. Add the fluid base to fill the cup up to the Max Line. Screw the Nutribullet Extractor Blade on to the top of the cup. Invert the cup, press it down into the Nutribullet Power Base and twist it into place. Blast the mixture until it is really smooth (20 or so seconds). **Enjoy!**

Yellow Pepper Splash

Ingredients

1 Cup/Handful of Green Cabbage (40 grams or 1½ oz)
1 Cup/Handful of Broccoli Florets (40 grams or 1½ oz)
1 Cup of Grapefruit segments (120 grams or 4 oz)
1 Cup of sliced Yellow Pepper (120 grams or 4 oz)
22 grams or ¾ oz of Flax Seeds
200 ml / 7 fl oz of Almond Milk (Unsweetened)

Protein 8g, Fat 12g, Carb 17g, Fibre 11g, 237 Kcals

Preparation

Place the nuts or seeds into the Tall Cup. Screw the Nutribullet Extractor Blade on to the top of the cup. Invert the cup, press it down into the Nutribullet Power Base and twist it into place. Blast them for 30 seconds. Put the rest of the solid ingredients into the cup and press them down below the Max Line. Add the fluid base to fill the cup up to the Max Line. Screw the Nutribullet Extractor Blade on to the top of the cup. Invert the cup, press it down into the Nutribullet Power Base and twist it into place. Blast the mixture until it is really smooth (20 or so seconds). **Enjoy!**

Guava and Hazelnut Elixir

Ingredients

1 Cup/Handful of Mint (40 grams or 1½ oz)
1 Cup/Handful of Fennel (40 grams or 1½ oz)
1 Cup of Guava (120 grams or 4 oz)
1 Cup of diced Beetroot (120 grams or 4 oz)
30 grams or 1 oz of Hazelnuts
200 ml / 7 fl oz of Coconut Milk

Protein 12g, Fat 22g, Carb 29g, Fibre 17g, 391 Kcals

Preparation

Place the nuts or seeds into the Tall Cup. Screw the Nutribullet Extractor Blade on to the top of the cup. Invert the cup, press it down into the Nutribullet Power Base and twist it into place. Blast them for 30 seconds. Put the rest of the solid ingredients into the cup and press them down below the Max Line. Add the fluid base to fill the cup up to the Max Line. Screw the Nutribullet Extractor Blade on to the top of the cup. Invert the cup, press it down into the Nutribullet Power Base and twist it into place. Blast the mixture until it is really smooth (20 or so seconds). **Enjoy!**

Broccoli Blockbuster

Ingredients

2 Cups/Handfuls of Broccoli Florets (80 grams or 3 oz)
1 Cup of Papaya (120 grams or 4 oz)
1 Cup of sliced Tomato (120 grams or 4 oz)
30 grams or 1 oz of Cashews
200 ml / 7 fl oz of Water

Protein 9g, Fat 14g, Carb 25g, Fibre 7g, 266 Kcals

Preparation

Place the nuts or seeds into the Tall Cup. Screw the Nutribullet Extractor Blade on to the top of the cup. Invert the cup, press it down into the Nutribullet Power Base and twist it into place. Blast them for 30 seconds. Put the rest of the solid ingredients into the cup and press them down below the Max Line. Add the fluid base to fill the cup up to the Max Line. Screw the Nutribullet Extractor Blade on to the top of the cup. Invert the cup, press it down into the Nutribullet Power Base and twist it into place. Blast the mixture until it is really smooth (20 or so seconds). **Enjoy!**

Bok Choy and Pecan Vortex

Ingredients

1 Cup/Handful of Red or White Cabbage (40 grams or 1½ oz)
1 Cup/Handful of Bok Choy (40 grams or 1½ oz)
1 Cup of Raspberries (120 grams or 4 oz)
1 Cup of sliced Fine Beans (120 grams or 4 oz)
30 grams or 1 oz of Pecans
200 ml / 7 fl oz of Half Fat Crème Fraiche

Protein 8g, Fat 53g, Carb 25g, Fibre 15g, 655 Kcals

Preparation

Place the nuts or seeds into the Tall Cup. Screw the Nutribullet Extractor Blade on to the top of the cup. Invert the cup, press it down into the Nutribullet Power Base and twist it into place. Blast them for 30 seconds. Put the rest of the solid ingredients into the cup and press them down below the Max Line. Add the fluid base to fill the cup up to the Max Line. Screw the Nutribullet Extractor Blade on to the top of the cup. Invert the cup, press it down into the Nutribullet Power Base and twist it into place. Blast the mixture until it is really smooth (20 or so seconds). **Enjoy!**

Tangerine and Sesame Journey

Ingredients

1 Cup/Handful of Rocket/Arugura Lettuce (40 grams or 1½ oz)
1 Cup/Handful of Lettuce Leaves (40 grams or 1½ oz)
1 Cup of Tangerine slices (120 grams or 4 oz)
1 Cup of Radishes (120 grams or 4 oz)
22 grams or ¾ oz of Sesame Seeds Hulled
200 ml / 7 fl oz of Dairy Milk Whole

Protein 13g, Fat 21g, Carb 27g, Fibre 7g, 355 Kcals

Preparation

Place the nuts or seeds into the Tall Cup. Screw the Nutribullet Extractor Blade on to the top of the cup. Invert the cup, press it down into the Nutribullet Power Base and twist it into place. Blast them for 30 seconds. Put the rest of the solid ingredients into the cup and press them down below the Max Line. Add the fluid base to fill the cup up to the Max Line. Screw the Nutribullet Extractor Blade on to the top of the cup. Invert the cup, press it down into the Nutribullet Power Base and twist it into place. Blast the mixture until it is really smooth (20 or so seconds). **Enjoy!**

Red Cabbage Rejunevator

Ingredients

1 Cup/Handful of Lettuce Leaves (40 grams or 1½ oz)
1 Cup/Handful of Red or White Cabbage (40 grams or 1½ oz)
1 Cup of Cherries (stoned) (120 grams or 4 oz)
1 Cup of sliced Zucchini/Courgette (120 grams or 4 oz)
30 grams or 1 oz of Peanuts
200 ml / 7 fl oz of Hazelnut Milk

Protein 12g, Fat 19g, Carb 30g, Fibre 9g, 343 Kcals

Preparation

Place the nuts or seeds into the Tall Cup. Screw the Nutribullet Extractor Blade on to the top of the cup. Invert the cup, press it down into the Nutribullet Power Base and twist it into place. Blast them for 30 seconds. Put the rest of the solid ingredients into the cup and press them down below the Max Line. Add the fluid base to fill the cup up to the Max Line. Screw the Nutribullet Extractor Blade on to the top of the cup. Invert the cup, press it down into the Nutribullet Power Base and twist it into place. Blast the mixture until it is really smooth (20 or so seconds). **Enjoy!**

Broccoli meets Walnut

Ingredients

1 Cup/Handful of Broccoli Florets (40 grams or 1½ oz)
1 Cup/Handful of Spinach (40 grams or 1½ oz)
1 Cup of Apricot halves (120 grams or 4 oz)
1 Cup of sliced Carrots (120 grams or 4 oz)
30 grams or 1 oz of Walnuts
200 ml / 7 fl oz of Water

Protein 10g, Fat 21g, Carb 23g, Fibre 10g, 325 Kcals

Preparation

Place the nuts or seeds into the Tall Cup. Screw the Nutribullet Extractor Blade on to the top of the cup. Invert the cup, press it down into the Nutribullet Power Base and twist it into place. Blast them for 30 seconds. Put the rest of the solid ingredients into the cup and press them down below the Max Line. Add the fluid base to fill the cup up to the Max Line. Screw the Nutribullet Extractor Blade on to the top of the cup. Invert the cup, press it down into the Nutribullet Power Base and twist it into place. Blast the mixture until it is really smooth (20 or so seconds). **Enjoy!**

Watercress and Cranberry Nectar

Ingredients

1 Cup/Handful of Watercress (40 grams or 1½ oz)
1 Cup/Handful of Fennel (40 grams or 1½ oz)
1 Cup of Cranberries (120 grams or 4 oz)
1 Cup of sliced Green Pepper (120 grams or 4 oz)
22 grams or ¾ oz of Pumpkin Seeds
200 ml / 7 fl oz of Half Fat Crème Fraiche

Protein 8g, Fat 40g, Carb 28g, Fibre 10g, 558 Kcals

Preparation

Place the nuts or seeds into the Tall Cup. Screw the Nutribullet Extractor Blade on to the top of the cup. Invert the cup, press it down into the Nutribullet Power Base and twist it into place. Blast them for 30 seconds. Put the rest of the solid ingredients into the cup and press them down below the Max Line. Add the fluid base to fill the cup up to the Max Line. Screw the Nutribullet Extractor Blade on to the top of the cup. Invert the cup, press it down into the Nutribullet Power Base and twist it into place. Blast the mixture until it is really smooth (20 or so seconds). **Enjoy!**

Water Melon and Almond Invigorator

Ingredients

1 Cup/Handful of Rocket/Arugura Lettuce (40 grams or 1½ oz)
1 Cup/Handful of Mint (40 grams or 1½ oz)
1 Cup of Water Melon chunks (120 grams or 4 oz)
1 Cup of diced Swede (120 grams or 4 oz)
30 grams or 1 oz of Almonds
200 ml / 7 fl oz of Hazelnut Milk

Protein 10g, Fat 20g, Carb 24g, Fibre 10g, 329 Kcals

Preparation

Place the nuts or seeds into the Tall Cup. Screw the Nutribullet Extractor Blade on to the top of the cup. Invert the cup, press it down into the Nutribullet Power Base and twist it into place. Blast them for 30 seconds. Put the rest of the solid ingredients into the cup and press them down below the Max Line. Add the fluid base to fill the cup up to the Max Line. Screw the Nutribullet Extractor Blade on to the top of the cup. Invert the cup, press it down into the Nutribullet Power Base and twist it into place. Blast the mixture until it is really smooth (20 or so seconds). **Enjoy!**

Mint goes Red Grape

Ingredients

2 Cups/Handfuls of Mint (80 grams or 3 oz)
1 Cup of Red Grapes (120 grams or 4 oz)
1 Cup of sliced Cauliflower florets (120 grams or 4 oz)
22 grams or ¾ oz of Sunflower Seeds Hulled
200 ml / 7 fl oz of Almond Milk (Unsweetened)

Protein 11g, Fat 14g, Carb 28g, Fibre 11g, 287 Kcals

Preparation

Place the nuts or seeds into the Tall Cup. Screw the Nutribullet Extractor Blade on to the top of the cup. Invert the cup, press it down into the Nutribullet Power Base and twist it into place. Blast them for 30 seconds. Put the rest of the solid ingredients into the cup and press them down below the Max Line. Add the fluid base to fill the cup up to the Max Line. Screw the Nutribullet Extractor Blade on to the top of the cup. Invert the cup, press it down into the Nutribullet Power Base and twist it into place. Blast the mixture until it is really smooth (20 or so seconds). **Enjoy!**

Brazil Bliss

Ingredients

1 Cup/Handful of Green Cabbage (40 grams or 1½ oz)
1 Cup/Handful of Bok Choy (40 grams or 1½ oz)
1 Cup of Strawberries (120 grams or 4 oz)
1 Cup of diced Turnip (120 grams or 4 oz)
30 grams or 1 oz of Brazil nuts
200 ml / 7 fl oz of Coconut Milk

Protein 7g, Fat 23g, Carb 21g, Fibre 8g, 324 Kcals

Preparation

Place the nuts or seeds into the Tall Cup. Screw the Nutribullet Extractor Blade on to the top of the cup. Invert the cup, press it down into the Nutribullet Power Base and twist it into place. Blast them for 30 seconds. Put the rest of the solid ingredients into the cup and press them down below the Max Line. Add the fluid base to fill the cup up to the Max Line. Screw the Nutribullet Extractor Blade on to the top of the cup. Invert the cup, press it down into the Nutribullet Power Base and twist it into place. Blast the mixture until it is really smooth (20 or so seconds). **Enjoy!**

Red Cabbage and Cashew Panacea

Ingredients

1 Cup/Handful of Red or White Cabbage (40 grams or 1½ oz)
1 Cup/Handful of Spinach (40 grams or 1½ oz)
1 small Banana (peeled and sliced) (120 grams or 4 oz)
1 Cup of sliced Cucumber (120 grams or 4 oz)
30 grams or 1 oz of Cashews
200 ml / 7 fl oz of Dairy Milk Whole

Protein 16g, Fat 21g, Carb 46g, Fibre 7g, 436 Kcals

Preparation

Place the nuts or seeds into the Tall Cup. Screw the Nutribullet Extractor Blade on to the top of the cup. Invert the cup, press it down into the Nutribullet Power Base and twist it into place. Blast them for 30 seconds. Put the rest of the solid ingredients into the cup and press them down below the Max Line. Add the fluid base to fill the cup up to the Max Line. Screw the Nutribullet Extractor Blade on to the top of the cup. Invert the cup, press it down into the Nutribullet Power Base and twist it into place. Blast the mixture until it is really smooth (20 or so seconds). **Enjoy!**

Rocket invites Apple

Ingredients

1 Cup/Handful of Green Cabbage (40 grams or 1½ oz)
1 Cup/Handful of Rocket/Arugura Lettuce (40 grams or 1½ oz)
1 small Apple (cored) (120 grams or 4 oz)
1 Cup of sliced Celery (120 grams or 4 oz)
30 grams or 1 oz of Almonds
200 ml / 7 fl oz of Greek Yoghurt

Protein 17g, Fat 35g, Carb 30g, Fibre 9g, 524 Kcals

Preparation

Place the nuts or seeds into the Tall Cup. Screw the Nutribullet Extractor Blade on to the top of the cup. Invert the cup, press it down into the Nutribullet Power Base and twist it into place. Blast them for 30 seconds. Put the rest of the solid ingredients into the cup and press them down below the Max Line. Add the fluid base to fill the cup up to the Max Line. Screw the Nutribullet Extractor Blade on to the top of the cup. Invert the cup, press it down into the Nutribullet Power Base and twist it into place. Blast the mixture until it is really smooth (20 or so seconds). **Enjoy!**

Red Pepper Rave

Ingredients

2 Cups/Handfuls of Watercress (80 grams or 3 oz)
1 Cup of Blueberries (120 grams or 4 oz)
1 Cup of sliced Red Pepper (120 grams or 4 oz)
30 grams or 1 oz of Pecans
200 ml / 7 fl oz of Almond Milk (Unsweetened)

Protein 7g, Fat 25g, Carb 21g, Fibre 9g, 347 Kcals

Preparation

Place the nuts or seeds into the Tall Cup. Screw the Nutribullet Extractor Blade on to the top of the cup. Invert the cup, press it down into the Nutribullet Power Base and twist it into place. Blast them for 30 seconds. Put the rest of the solid ingredients into the cup and press them down below the Max Line. Add the fluid base to fill the cup up to the Max Line. Screw the Nutribullet Extractor Blade on to the top of the cup. Invert the cup, press it down into the Nutribullet Power Base and twist it into place. Blast the mixture until it is really smooth (20 or so seconds). **Enjoy!**

Mint loves Peanut

Ingredients

1 Cup/Handful of Fennel (40 grams or 1½ oz)
1 Cup/Handful of Mint (40 grams or 1½ oz)
½ Cup of Goji Berries Dried (40 grams or 1½ oz)
1 Cup of diced Turnip (120 grams or 4 oz)
30 grams or 1 oz of Peanuts
200 ml / 7 fl oz of Water

Protein 16g, Fat 16g, Carb 33g, Fibre 11g, 362 Kcals

Preparation

Place the nuts or seeds into the Tall Cup. Screw the Nutribullet Extractor Blade on to the top of the cup. Invert the cup, press it down into the Nutribullet Power Base and twist it into place. Blast them for 30 seconds. Put the rest of the solid ingredients into the cup and press them down below the Max Line. Add the fluid base to fill the cup up to the Max Line. Screw the Nutribullet Extractor Blade on to the top of the cup. Invert the cup, press it down into the Nutribullet Power Base and twist it into place. Blast the mixture until it is really smooth (20 or so seconds). **Enjoy!**

Watercress and Hazelnut Potion

Ingredients

1 Cup/Handful of Bok Choy (40 grams or 1½ oz)
1 Cup/Handful of Watercress (40 grams or 1½ oz)
1 Cup of Orange segments (120 grams or 4 oz)
1 Cup of sliced Cauliflower florets (120 grams or 4 oz)
30 grams or 1 oz of Hazelnuts
200 ml / 7 fl oz of Coconut Milk

Protein 10g, Fat 21g, Carb 23g, Fibre 9g, 324 Kcals

Preparation

Place the nuts or seeds into the Tall Cup. Screw the Nutribullet Extractor Blade on to the top of the cup. Invert the cup, press it down into the Nutribullet Power Base and twist it into place. Blast them for 30 seconds. Put the rest of the solid ingredients into the cup and press them down below the Max Line. Add the fluid base to fill the cup up to the Max Line. Screw the Nutribullet Extractor Blade on to the top of the cup. Invert the cup, press it down into the Nutribullet Power Base and twist it into place. Blast the mixture until it is really smooth (20 or so seconds). **Enjoy!**

Swede Symphony

Ingredients

1 Cup/Handful of Broccoli Florets (40 grams or 1½ oz)
1 Cup/Handful of Lettuce Leaves (40 grams or 1½ oz)
1 Cup of Prunes (stoned) (120 grams or 4 oz)
1 Cup of diced Swede (120 grams or 4 oz)
22 grams or ¾ oz of Flax Seeds
200 ml / 7 fl oz of Half Fat Crème Fraiche

Protein 8g, Fat 42g, Carb 23g, Fibre 13g, 515 Kcals

Preparation

Place the nuts or seeds into the Tall Cup. Screw the Nutribullet Extractor Blade on to the top of the cup. Invert the cup, press it down into the Nutribullet Power Base and twist it into place. Blast them for 30 seconds. Put the rest of the solid ingredients into the cup and press them down below the Max Line. Add the fluid base to fill the cup up to the Max Line. Screw the Nutribullet Extractor Blade on to the top of the cup. Invert the cup, press it down into the Nutribullet Power Base and twist it into place. Blast the mixture until it is really smooth (20 or so seconds). **Enjoy!**

Watercress Therapy

Ingredients

1 Cup/Handful of Red or White Cabbage (40 grams or 1½ oz)
1 Cup/Handful of Watercress (40 grams or 1½ oz)
1 Cup of Peach slices (120 grams or 4 oz)
1 Cup of sliced Red Pepper (120 grams or 4 oz)
22 grams or ¾ oz of Sunflower Seeds Hulled
200 ml / 7 fl oz of Hazelnut Milk

Protein 9g, Fat 14g, Carb 26g, Fibre 7g, 272 Kcals

Preparation

Place the nuts or seeds into the Tall Cup. Screw the Nutribullet Extractor Blade on to the top of the cup. Invert the cup, press it down into the Nutribullet Power Base and twist it into place. Blast them for 30 seconds. Put the rest of the solid ingredients into the cup and press them down below the Max Line. Add the fluid base to fill the cup up to the Max Line. Screw the Nutribullet Extractor Blade on to the top of the cup. Invert the cup, press it down into the Nutribullet Power Base and twist it into place. Blast the mixture until it is really smooth (20 or so seconds). **Enjoy!**

Blackberry and Radish Embrace

Ingredients

2 Cups/Handfuls of Green Cabbage (80 grams or 3 oz)
1 Cup of Blackberries (120 grams or 4 oz)
1 Cup of Radishes (120 grams or 4 oz)
30 grams or 1 oz of Walnuts
200 ml / 7 fl oz of Dairy Milk Whole

Protein 14g, Fat 28g, Carb 21g, Fibre 12g, 414 Kcals

Preparation

Place the nuts or seeds into the Tall Cup. Screw the Nutribullet Extractor Blade on to the top of the cup. Invert the cup, press it down into the Nutribullet Power Base and twist it into place. Blast them for 30 seconds. Put the rest of the solid ingredients into the cup and press them down below the Max Line. Add the fluid base to fill the cup up to the Max Line. Screw the Nutribullet Extractor Blade on to the top of the cup. Invert the cup, press it down into the Nutribullet Power Base and twist it into place. Blast the mixture until it is really smooth (20 or so seconds). **Enjoy!**

Pear goes Pumpkin

Ingredients

2 Cups/Handfuls of Bok Choy (80 grams or 3 oz)
1 small Pear (cored) (120 grams or 4 oz)
1 Cup of diced Celeriac (120 grams or 4 oz)
22 grams or ¾ oz of Pumpkin Seeds
200 ml / 7 fl oz of Greek Yoghurt

Protein 17g, Fat 29g, Carb 39g, Fibre 8g, 503 Kcals

Preparation

Place the nuts or seeds into the Tall Cup. Screw the Nutribullet Extractor Blade on to the top of the cup. Invert the cup, press it down into the Nutribullet Power Base and twist it into place. Blast them for 30 seconds. Put the rest of the solid ingredients into the cup and press them down below the Max Line. Add the fluid base to fill the cup up to the Max Line. Screw the Nutribullet Extractor Blade on to the top of the cup. Invert the cup, press it down into the Nutribullet Power Base and twist it into place. Blast the mixture until it is really smooth (20 or so seconds). **Enjoy!**

Avocado Avenue

Ingredients

2 Cups/Handfuls of Broccoli Florets (80 grams or 3 oz)
1 small Avocado (stoned and peeled) (120 grams or 4 oz)
1 Cup of sliced Yellow Pepper (120 grams or 4 oz)
30 grams or 1 oz of Brazil nuts
200 ml / 7 fl oz of Almond Milk (Unsweetened)

Protein 11g, Fat 40g, Carb 12g, Fibre 14g, 475 Kcals

Preparation

Place the nuts or seeds into the Tall Cup. Screw the Nutribullet Extractor Blade on to the top of the cup. Invert the cup, press it down into the Nutribullet Power Base and twist it into place. Blast them for 30 seconds. Put the rest of the solid ingredients into the cup and press them down below the Max Line. Add the fluid base to fill the cup up to the Max Line. Screw the Nutribullet Extractor Blade on to the top of the cup. Invert the cup, press it down into the Nutribullet Power Base and twist it into place. Blast the mixture until it is really smooth (20 or so seconds). **Enjoy!**

Broccoli in Nectarine

Ingredients

1 Cup/Handful of Green Cabbage (40 grams or 1½ oz)
1 Cup/Handful of Broccoli Florets (40 grams or 1½ oz)
1 Cup of Nectarine segments (120 grams or 4 oz)
1 Cup of sliced Celery (120 grams or 4 oz)
22 grams or ¾ oz of Sesame Seeds Hulled
200 ml / 7 fl oz of Hazelnut Milk

Protein 8g, Fat 17g, Carb 21g, Fibre 8g, 285 Kcals

Preparation

Place the nuts or seeds into the Tall Cup. Screw the Nutribullet Extractor Blade on to the top of the cup. Invert the cup, press it down into the Nutribullet Power Base and twist it into place. Blast them for 30 seconds. Put the rest of the solid ingredients into the cup and press them down below the Max Line. Add the fluid base to fill the cup up to the Max Line. Screw the Nutribullet Extractor Blade on to the top of the cup. Invert the cup, press it down into the Nutribullet Power Base and twist it into place. Blast the mixture until it is really smooth (20 or so seconds). **Enjoy!**

Fennel in Chia

Ingredients

1 Cup/Handful of Fennel (40 grams or 1½ oz)
1 Cup/Handful of Lettuce Leaves (40 grams or 1½ oz)
1 Cup of Clementine slices (120 grams or 4 oz)
1 Cup of sliced Green Pepper (120 grams or 4 oz)
22 grams or ¾ oz of Chia Seeds
200 ml / 7 fl oz of Coconut Milk

Protein 7g, Fat 9g, Carb 25g, Fibre 14g, 246 Kcals

Preparation

Place the nuts or seeds into the Tall Cup. Screw the Nutribullet Extractor Blade on to the top of the cup. Invert the cup, press it down into the Nutribullet Power Base and twist it into place. Blast them for 30 seconds. Put the rest of the solid ingredients into the cup and press them down below the Max Line. Add the fluid base to fill the cup up to the Max Line. Screw the Nutribullet Extractor Blade on to the top of the cup. Invert the cup, press it down into the Nutribullet Power Base and twist it into place. Blast the mixture until it is really smooth (20 or so seconds). **Enjoy!**

Spinach joins Cashew

Ingredients

1 Cup/Handful of Bok Choy (40 grams or 1½ oz)
1 Cup/Handful of Spinach (40 grams or 1½ oz)
1 Cup of Dates (stoned) (120 grams or 4 oz)
1 Cup of diced Beetroot (120 grams or 4 oz)
30 grams or 1 oz of Cashews
200 ml / 7 fl oz of Half Fat Crème Fraiche

Protein 12g, Fat 44g, Carb 109g, Fibre 15g, 908 Kcals

Preparation

Place the nuts or seeds into the Tall Cup. Screw the Nutribullet Extractor Blade on to the top of the cup. Invert the cup, press it down into the Nutribullet Power Base and twist it into place. Blast them for 30 seconds. Put the rest of the solid ingredients into the cup and press them down below the Max Line. Add the fluid base to fill the cup up to the Max Line. Screw the Nutribullet Extractor Blade on to the top of the cup. Invert the cup, press it down into the Nutribullet Power Base and twist it into place. Blast the mixture until it is really smooth (20 or so seconds). **Enjoy!**

Classic Smoothies

Mint Medley

Ingredients

1 Cup/Handful of Bok Choy (40 grams or 1½ oz)
1 Cup/Handful of Mint (40 grams or 1½ oz)
2 Cups of Peeled Figs (240 grams or 8 oz)
200 ml / 7 fl oz of Greek Yoghurt

Protein 12g, Fat 20g, Carb 51g, Fibre 10g, 450 Kcals

Preparation

Put all the solid ingredients into the Tall Cup and press them down below the Max Line. Add the fluid base to fill the cup up to the Max Line. Screw the Nutribullet Extractor Blade on to the top of the cup. Invert the cup, press it down into the Nutribullet Power Base and twist it into place. Blast the mixture until it is really smooth (20 or so seconds). **Enjoy!**

Lettuce Nectar

Ingredients

2 Cups/Handfuls of Lettuce Leaves (80 grams or 3 oz)
1 Cup of Water Melon chunks (120 grams or 4 oz)
1 small Pear (cored) (120 grams or 4 oz)
200 ml / 7 fl oz of Half Fat Crème Fraiche

Protein 2g, Fat 31g, Carb 36g, Fibre 6g, 455 Kcals

Preparation

Put all the solid ingredients into the Tall Cup and press them down below the Max Line. Add the fluid base to fill the cup up to the Max Line. Screw the Nutribullet Extractor Blade on to the top of the cup. Invert the cup, press it down into the Nutribullet Power Base and twist it into place. Blast the mixture until it is really smooth (20 or so seconds). **Enjoy!**

Watercress and Orange is lovely

Ingredients

1 Cup/Handful of Lettuce Leaves (40 grams or 1½ oz)
1 Cup/Handful of Watercress (40 grams or 1½ oz)
1 Cup of Papaya (120 grams or 4 oz)
1 Cup of Orange segments (120 grams or 4 oz)
200 ml / 7 fl oz of Dairy Milk Whole

Protein 10g, Fat 8g, Carb 32g, Fibre 6g, 247 Kcals

Preparation

Put all the solid ingredients into the Tall Cup and press them down below the Max Line. Add the fluid base to fill the cup up to the Max Line. Screw the Nutribullet Extractor Blade on to the top of the cup. Invert the cup, press it down into the Nutribullet Power Base and twist it into place. Blast the mixture until it is really smooth (20 or so seconds). **Enjoy!**

Bok Choy needs Red Grape

Ingredients

2 Cups/Handfuls of Bok Choy (80 grams or 3 oz)
1 Cup of Red Grapes (120 grams or 4 oz)
½ Cup of Goji Berries Dried (40 grams or 1½ oz)
200 ml / 7 fl oz of Water

Protein 8g, Fat 1g, Carb 44g, Fibre 4g, 221 Kcals

Preparation

Put all the solid ingredients into the Tall Cup and press them down below the Max Line. Add the fluid base to fill the cup up to the Max Line. Screw the Nutribullet Extractor Blade on to the top of the cup. Invert the cup, press it down into the Nutribullet Power Base and twist it into place. Blast the mixture until it is really smooth (20 or so seconds). **Enjoy!**

Guava Revelation

Ingredients

2 Cups/Handfuls of Fennel (80 grams or 3 oz)
1 Cup of Guava (120 grams or 4 oz)
1 Cup of Blueberries (120 grams or 4 oz)
200 ml / 7 fl oz of Almond Milk (Unsweetened)

Protein 6g, Fat 4g, Carb 29g, Fibre 13g, 200 Kcals

Preparation

Put all the solid ingredients into the Tall Cup and press them down below the Max Line. Add the fluid base to fill the cup up to the Max Line. Screw the Nutribullet Extractor Blade on to the top of the cup. Invert the cup, press it down into the Nutribullet Power Base and twist it into place. Blast the mixture until it is really smooth (20 or so seconds). **Enjoy!**

Avocado Mirage

Ingredients

1 Cup/Handful of Rocket/Arugura Lettuce (40 grams or 1½ oz)
1 Cup/Handful of Green Cabbage (40 grams or 1½ oz)
1 small Banana (peeled and sliced) (120 grams or 4 oz)
1 small Avocado (stoned and peeled) (120 grams or 4 oz)
200 ml / 7 fl oz of Hazelnut Milk

Protein 5g, Fat 21g, Carb 34g, Fibre 13g, 372 Kcals

Preparation

Put all the solid ingredients into the Tall Cup and press them down below the Max Line. Add the fluid base to fill the cup up to the Max Line. Screw the Nutribullet Extractor Blade on to the top of the cup. Invert the cup, press it down into the Nutribullet Power Base and twist it into place. Blast the mixture until it is really smooth (20 or so seconds). **Enjoy!**

Broccoli and Apricot Snog

Ingredients

1 Cup/Handful of Spinach (40 grams or 1½ oz)
1 Cup/Handful of Broccoli Florets (40 grams or 1½ oz)
1 Cup of Apricot halves (120 grams or 4 oz)
1 Cup of Grapefruit segments (120 grams or 4 oz)
200 ml / 7 fl oz of Coconut Milk

Protein 5g, Fat 3g, Carb 27g, Fibre 6g, 158 Kcals

Preparation

Put all the solid ingredients into the Tall Cup and press them down below the Max Line. Add the fluid base to fill the cup up to the Max Line. Screw the Nutribullet Extractor Blade on to the top of the cup. Invert the cup, press it down into the Nutribullet Power Base and twist it into place. Blast the mixture until it is really smooth (20 or so seconds). **Enjoy!**

Fennel and Pineapple Waistline

Ingredients

1 Cup/Handful of Red or White Cabbage (40 grams or 1½ oz)
1 Cup/Handful of Fennel (40 grams or 1½ oz)
2 Cups of Pineapple chunks (240 grams or 8 oz)
200 ml / 7 fl oz of Dairy Milk Whole

Protein 9g, Fat 8g, Carb 41g, Fibre 5g, 272 Kcals

Preparation

Put all the solid ingredients into the Tall Cup and press them down below the Max Line. Add the fluid base to fill the cup up to the Max Line. Screw the Nutribullet Extractor Blade on to the top of the cup. Invert the cup, press it down into the Nutribullet Power Base and twist it into place. Blast the mixture until it is really smooth (20 or so seconds). **Enjoy!**

Fennel Fantasy

Ingredients

1 Cup/Handful of Fennel (40 grams or 1½ oz)
1 Cup/Handful of Spinach (40 grams or 1½ oz)
1 Cup of Clementine slices (120 grams or 4 oz)
1 Cup of Dates (stoned) (120 grams or 4 oz)
200 ml / 7 fl oz of Hazelnut Milk

Protein 6g, Fat 4g, Carb 101g, Fibre 14g, 474 Kcals

Preparation

Put all the solid ingredients into the Tall Cup and press them down below the Max Line. Add the fluid base to fill the cup up to the Max Line. Screw the Nutribullet Extractor Blade on to the top of the cup. Invert the cup, press it down into the Nutribullet Power Base and twist it into place. Blast the mixture until it is really smooth (20 or so seconds). **Enjoy!**

Green Cabbage loves Kiwi

Ingredients

2 Cups/Handfuls of Green Cabbage (80 grams or 3 oz)
1 Cup of Kiwi Fruit slices (120 grams or 4 oz)
1 Cup of Blackberries (120 grams or 4 oz)
200 ml / 7 fl oz of Water

Protein 4g, Fat 1g, Carb 22g, Fibre 12g, 144 Kcals

Preparation

Put all the solid ingredients into the Tall Cup and press them down below the Max Line. Add the fluid base to fill the cup up to the Max Line. Screw the Nutribullet Extractor Blade on to the top of the cup. Invert the cup, press it down into the Nutribullet Power Base and twist it into place. Blast the mixture until it is really smooth (20 or so seconds). **Enjoy!**

Rocket embraces Blackberry

Ingredients

1 Cup/Handful of Green Cabbage (40 grams or 1½ oz)
1 Cup/Handful of Rocket/Arugura Lettuce (40 grams or 1½ oz)
2 Cups of Blackberries (240 grams or 8 oz)
200 ml / 7 fl oz of Almond Milk (Unsweetened)

Protein 5g, Fat 3g, Carb 12g, Fibre 15g, 145 Kcals

Preparation

Put all the solid ingredients into the Tall Cup and press them down below the Max Line. Add the fluid base to fill the cup up to the Max Line. Screw the Nutribullet Extractor Blade on to the top of the cup. Invert the cup, press it down into the Nutribullet Power Base and twist it into place. Blast the mixture until it is really smooth (20 or so seconds). **Enjoy!**

Mint loves Apricot

Ingredients

1 Cup/Handful of Mint (40 grams or 1½ oz)
1 Cup/Handful of Broccoli Florets (40 grams or 1½ oz)
2 Cups of Apricot halves (240 grams or 8 oz)
200 ml / 7 fl oz of Coconut Milk

Protein 6g, Fat 3g, Carb 30g, Fibre 9g, 186 Kcals

Preparation

Put all the solid ingredients into the Tall Cup and press them down below the Max Line. Add the fluid base to fill the cup up to the Max Line. Screw the Nutribullet Extractor Blade on to the top of the cup. Invert the cup, press it down into the Nutribullet Power Base and twist it into place. Blast the mixture until it is really smooth (20 or so seconds). **Enjoy!**

Bok Choy in Nectarine

Ingredients

1 Cup/Handful of Watercress (40 grams or 1½ oz)
1 Cup/Handful of Bok Choy (40 grams or 1½ oz)
1 Cup of Nectarine segments (120 grams or 4 oz)
1 Cup of Cherries (stoned) (120 grams or 4 oz)
200 ml / 7 fl oz of Greek Yoghurt

Protein 12g, Fat 20g, Carb 39g, Fibre 5g, 387 Kcals

Preparation

Put all the solid ingredients into the Tall Cup and press them down below the Max Line. Add the fluid base to fill the cup up to the Max Line. Screw the Nutribullet Extractor Blade on to the top of the cup. Invert the cup, press it down into the Nutribullet Power Base and twist it into place. Blast the mixture until it is really smooth (20 or so seconds). **Enjoy!**

Red Cabbage and Cranberry Booster

Ingredients

1 Cup/Handful of Red or White Cabbage (40 grams or 1½ oz)
1 Cup/Handful of Lettuce Leaves (40 grams or 1½ oz)
1 Cup of Cranberries (120 grams or 4 oz)
1 Cup of Pineapple chunks (120 grams or 4 oz)
200 ml / 7 fl oz of Half Fat Crème Fraiche

Protein 2g, Fat 30g, Carb 37g, Fibre 9g, 472 Kcals

Preparation

Put all the solid ingredients into the Tall Cup and press them down below the Max Line. Add the fluid base to fill the cup up to the Max Line. Screw the Nutribullet Extractor Blade on to the top of the cup. Invert the cup, press it down into the Nutribullet Power Base and twist it into place. Blast the mixture until it is really smooth (20 or so seconds). **Enjoy!**

Strawberry and Peach Extracted

Ingredients

2 Cups/Handfuls of Mint (80 grams or 3 oz)
1 Cup of Strawberries (120 grams or 4 oz)
1 Cup of Peach slices (120 grams or 4 oz)
200 ml / 7 fl oz of Hazelnut Milk

Protein 5g, Fat 4g, Carb 24g, Fibre 10g, 178 Kcals

Preparation

Put all the solid ingredients into the Tall Cup and press them down below the Max Line. Add the fluid base to fill the cup up to the Max Line. Screw the Nutribullet Extractor Blade on to the top of the cup. Invert the cup, press it down into the Nutribullet Power Base and twist it into place. Blast the mixture until it is really smooth (20 or so seconds). **Enjoy!**

Spinach Sensation

Ingredients

1 Cup/Handful of Bok Choy (40 grams or 1½ oz)
1 Cup/Handful of Spinach (40 grams or 1½ oz)
1 Cup of Plum halves (120 grams or 4 oz)
1 Cup of Tangerine slices (120 grams or 4 oz)
200 ml / 7 fl oz of Coconut Milk

Protein 4g, Fat 3g, Carb 32g, Fibre 5g, 173 Kcals

Preparation

Put all the solid ingredients into the Tall Cup and press them down below the Max Line. Add the fluid base to fill the cup up to the Max Line. Screw the Nutribullet Extractor Blade on to the top of the cup. Invert the cup, press it down into the Nutribullet Power Base and twist it into place. Blast the mixture until it is really smooth (20 or so seconds). **Enjoy!**

Green Cabbage and Melon Machine

Ingredients

1 Cup/Handful of Green Cabbage (40 grams or 1½ oz)
1 Cup/Handful of Mint (40 grams or 1½ oz)
1 Cup of Mango slices (120 grams or 4 oz)
1 Cup of Melon chunks (120 grams or 4 oz)
200 ml / 7 fl oz of Water

Protein 3g, Fat 1.0g, Carb 28g, Fibre 7g, 142 Kcals

Preparation

Put all the solid ingredients into the Tall Cup and press them down below the Max Line. Add the fluid base to fill the cup up to the Max Line. Screw the Nutribullet Extractor Blade on to the top of the cup. Invert the cup, press it down into the Nutribullet Power Base and twist it into place. Blast the mixture until it is really smooth (20 or so seconds). **Enjoy!**

Watercress in Plum

Ingredients

2 Cups/Handfuls of Watercress (80 grams or 3 oz)
2 Cups of Plum halves (240 grams or 8 oz)
200 ml / 7 fl oz of Dairy Milk Whole

Protein 10g, Fat 8g, Carb 34g, Fibre 4g, 247 Kcals

Preparation

Put all the solid ingredients into the Tall Cup and press them down below the Max Line. Add the fluid base to fill the cup up to the Max Line. Screw the Nutribullet Extractor Blade on to the top of the cup. Invert the cup, press it down into the Nutribullet Power Base and twist it into place. Blast the mixture until it is really smooth (20 or so seconds). **Enjoy!**

Red Cabbage and Peeled Fig Concerto

Ingredients

1 Cup/Handful of Red or White Cabbage (40 grams or 1½ oz)
1 Cup/Handful of Broccoli Florets (40 grams or 1½ oz)
1 Cup of Peeled Figs (120 grams or 4 oz)
1 small Apple (cored) (120 grams or 4 oz)
200 ml / 7 fl oz of Almond Milk (Unsweetened)

Protein 4g, Fat 3g, Carb 37g, Fibre 9g, 203 Kcals

Preparation

Put all the solid ingredients into the Tall Cup and press them down below the Max Line. Add the fluid base to fill the cup up to the Max Line. Screw the Nutribullet Extractor Blade on to the top of the cup. Invert the cup, press it down into the Nutribullet Power Base and twist it into place. Blast the mixture until it is really smooth (20 or so seconds). **Enjoy!**

Lettuce and Prune Reaction

Ingredients

1 Cup/Handful of Fennel (40 grams or 1½ oz)
1 Cup/Handful of Lettuce Leaves (40 grams or 1½ oz)
1 Cup of Raspberries (120 grams or 4 oz)
1 Cup of Prunes (stoned) (120 grams or 4 oz)
200 ml / 7 fl oz of Half Fat Crème Fraiche

Protein 4g, Fat 33g, Carb 24g, Fibre 13g, 424 Kcals

Preparation

Put all the solid ingredients into the Tall Cup and press them down below the Max Line. Add the fluid base to fill the cup up to the Max Line. Screw the Nutribullet Extractor Blade on to the top of the cup. Invert the cup, press it down into the Nutribullet Power Base and twist it into place. Blast the mixture until it is really smooth (20 or so seconds). **Enjoy!**

Mango Tango

Ingredients

1 Cup/Handful of Watercress (40 grams or 1½ oz)
1 Cup/Handful of Rocket/Arugura Lettuce (40 grams or 1½ oz)
1 Cup of Kiwi Fruit slices (120 grams or 4 oz)
1 Cup of Mango slices (120 grams or 4 oz)
200 ml / 7 fl oz of Greek Yoghurt

Protein 12g, Fat 20g, Carb 42g, Fibre 6g, 405 Kcals

Preparation

Put all the solid ingredients into the Tall Cup and press them down below the Max Line. Add the fluid base to fill the cup up to the Max Line. Screw the Nutribullet Extractor Blade on to the top of the cup. Invert the cup, press it down into the Nutribullet Power Base and twist it into place. Blast the mixture until it is really smooth (20 or so seconds). **Enjoy!**

Cherry Berry

Ingredients

1 Cup/Handful of Rocket/Arugura Lettuce (40 grams or 1½ oz)
1 Cup/Handful of Fennel (40 grams or 1½ oz)
1 Cup of Cherries (stoned) (120 grams or 4 oz)
1 Cup of Raspberries (120 grams or 4 oz)
200 ml / 7 fl oz of Almond Milk (Unsweetened)

Protein 5g, Fat 3g, Carb 26g, Fibre 13g, 182 Kcals

Preparation

Put all the solid ingredients into the Tall Cup and press them down below the Max Line. Add the fluid base to fill the cup up to the Max Line. Screw the Nutribullet Extractor Blade on to the top of the cup. Invert the cup, press it down into the Nutribullet Power Base and twist it into place. Blast the mixture until it is really smooth (20 or so seconds). **Enjoy!**

Red Cabbage meets Melon

Ingredients

1 Cup/Handful of Mint (40 grams or 1½ oz)
1 Cup/Handful of Red or White Cabbage (40 grams or 1½ oz)
2 Cups of Melon chunks (240 grams or 8 oz)
200 ml / 7 fl oz of Greek Yoghurt

Protein 12g, Fat 20g, Carb 34g, Fibre 5g, 366 Kcals

Preparation

Put all the solid ingredients into the Tall Cup and press them down below the Max Line. Add the fluid base to fill the cup up to the Max Line. Screw the Nutribullet Extractor Blade on to the top of the cup. Invert the cup, press it down into the Nutribullet Power Base and twist it into place. Blast the mixture until it is really smooth (20 or so seconds). **Enjoy!**

Spinach and Papaya Concerto

Ingredients

1 Cup/Handful of Spinach (40 grams or 1½ oz)
1 Cup/Handful of Lettuce Leaves (40 grams or 1½ oz)
2 Cups of Papaya (240 grams or 8 oz)
200 ml / 7 fl oz of Coconut Milk

Protein 3g, Fat 3g, Carb 28g, Fibre 6g, 159 Kcals

Preparation

Put all the solid ingredients into the Tall Cup and press them down below the Max Line. Add the fluid base to fill the cup up to the Max Line. Screw the Nutribullet Extractor Blade on to the top of the cup. Invert the cup, press it down into the Nutribullet Power Base and twist it into place. Blast the mixture until it is really smooth (20 or so seconds). **Enjoy!**

Mint goes Clementine

Ingredients

2 Cups/Handfuls of Mint (80 grams or 3 oz)
2 Cups of Clementine slices (240 grams or 8 oz)
200 ml / 7 fl oz of Water

Protein 5g, Fat 0.9g, Carb 26g, Fibre 10g, 147 Kcals

Preparation

Put all the solid ingredients into the Tall Cup and press them down below the Max Line. Add the fluid base to fill the cup up to the Max Line. Screw the Nutribullet Extractor Blade on to the top of the cup. Invert the cup, press it down into the Nutribullet Power Base and twist it into place. Blast the mixture until it is really smooth (20 or so seconds). **Enjoy!**

Date Kiss

Ingredients

2 Cups/Handfuls of Mint (80 grams or 3 oz)
1 Cup of Dates (stoned) (120 grams or 4 oz)
1 Cup of sliced Cucumber (120 grams or 4 oz)
200 ml / 7 fl oz of Greek Yoghurt

Protein 15g, Fat 20g, Carb 94g, Fibre 16g, 637 Kcals

Preparation

Put all the solid ingredients into the Tall Cup and press them down below the Max Line. Add the fluid base to fill the cup up to the Max Line. Screw the Nutribullet Extractor Blade on to the top of the cup. Invert the cup, press it down into the Nutribullet Power Base and twist it into place. Blast the mixture until it is really smooth (20 or so seconds). **Enjoy!**

Carrot Tonic

Ingredients

1 Cup/Handful of Green Cabbage (40 grams or 1½ oz)
1 Cup/Handful of Bok Choy (40 grams or 1½ oz)
1 Cup of Mango slices (120 grams or 4 oz)
1 Cup of sliced Carrots (120 grams or 4 oz)
200 ml / 7 fl oz of Half Fat Crème Fraiche

Protein 3g, Fat 31g, Carb 37g, Fibre 7g, 474 Kcals

Preparation

Put all the solid ingredients into the Tall Cup and press them down below the Max Line. Add the fluid base to fill the cup up to the Max Line. Screw the Nutribullet Extractor Blade on to the top of the cup. Invert the cup, press it down into the Nutribullet Power Base and twist it into place. Blast the mixture until it is really smooth (20 or so seconds). **Enjoy!**

Beetroot Blossom

Ingredients

1 Cup/Handful of Lettuce Leaves (40 grams or 1½ oz)
1 Cup/Handful of Red or White Cabbage (40 grams or 1½ oz)
1 Cup of Water Melon chunks (120 grams or 4 oz)
1 Cup of diced Beetroot (120 grams or 4 oz)
200 ml / 7 fl oz of Coconut Milk

Protein 4g, Fat 2g, Carb 25g, Fibre 6g, 146 Kcals

Preparation

Put all the solid ingredients into the Tall Cup and press them down below the Max Line. Add the fluid base to fill the cup up to the Max Line. Screw the Nutribullet Extractor Blade on to the top of the cup. Invert the cup, press it down into the Nutribullet Power Base and twist it into place. Blast the mixture until it is really smooth (20 or so seconds). **Enjoy!**

Celeriac Constellation

Ingredients

1 Cup/Handful of Watercress (40 grams or 1½ oz)
1 Cup/Handful of Broccoli Florets (40 grams or 1½ oz)
½ Cup of Goji Berries Dried (40 grams or 1½ oz)
1 Cup of diced Celeriac (120 grams or 4 oz)
200 ml / 7 fl oz of Water

Protein 9g, Fat 1g, Carb 34g, Fibre 5g, 196 Kcals

Preparation

Put all the solid ingredients into the Tall Cup and press them down below the Max Line. Add the fluid base to fill the cup up to the Max Line. Screw the Nutribullet Extractor Blade on to the top of the cup. Invert the cup, press it down into the Nutribullet Power Base and twist it into place. Blast the mixture until it is really smooth (20 or so seconds). **Enjoy!**

Rocket Rush

Ingredients

1 Cup/Handful of Mint (40 grams or 1½ oz)
1 Cup/Handful of Rocket/Arugura Lettuce (40 grams or 1½ oz)
1 Cup of Guava (120 grams or 4 oz)
1 Cup of sliced Fine Beans (120 grams or 4 oz)
200 ml / 7 fl oz of Almond Milk (Unsweetened)

Protein 8g, Fat 4g, Carb 16g, Fibre 13g, 161 Kcals

Preparation

Put all the solid ingredients into the Tall Cup and press them down below the Max Line. Add the fluid base to fill the cup up to the Max Line. Screw the Nutribullet Extractor Blade on to the top of the cup. Invert the cup, press it down into the Nutribullet Power Base and twist it into place. Blast the mixture until it is really smooth (20 or so seconds). **Enjoy!**

Spinach Splendour

Ingredients

1 Cup/Handful of Fennel (40 grams or 1½ oz)
1 Cup/Handful of Spinach (40 grams or 1½ oz)
1 Cup of Melon chunks (120 grams or 4 oz)
1 Cup of sliced Celery (120 grams or 4 oz)
200 ml / 7 fl oz of Dairy Milk Whole

Protein 10g, Fat 8g, Carb 23g, Fibre 5g, 211 Kcals

Preparation

Put all the solid ingredients into the Tall Cup and press them down below the Max Line. Add the fluid base to fill the cup up to the Max Line. Screw the Nutribullet Extractor Blade on to the top of the cup. Invert the cup, press it down into the Nutribullet Power Base and twist it into place. Blast the mixture until it is really smooth (20 or so seconds). **Enjoy!**

Papaya Royale

Ingredients

2 Cups/Handfuls of Green Cabbage (80 grams or 3 oz)
1 Cup of Papaya (120 grams or 4 oz)
1 Cup of sliced Zucchini/Courgette (120 grams or 4 oz)
200 ml / 7 fl oz of Hazelnut Milk

Protein 4g, Fat 4g, Carb 22g, Fibre 6g, 150 Kcals

Preparation

Put all the solid ingredients into the Tall Cup and press them down below the Max Line. Add the fluid base to fill the cup up to the Max Line. Screw the Nutribullet Extractor Blade on to the top of the cup. Invert the cup, press it down into the Nutribullet Power Base and twist it into place. Blast the mixture until it is really smooth (20 or so seconds). **Enjoy!**

Lettuce and Pineapple Infusion

Ingredients

1 Cup/Handful of Lettuce Leaves (40 grams or 1½ oz)
1 Cup/Handful of Rocket/Arugura Lettuce (40 grams or 1½ oz)
1 Cup of Pineapple chunks (120 grams or 4 oz)
1 Cup of sliced Cauliflower florets (120 grams or 4 oz)
200 ml / 7 fl oz of Water

Protein 4g, Fat 0.7g, Carb 19g, Fibre 5g, 102 Kcals

Preparation

Put all the solid ingredients into the Tall Cup and press them down below the Max Line. Add the fluid base to fill the cup up to the Max Line. Screw the Nutribullet Extractor Blade on to the top of the cup. Invert the cup, press it down into the Nutribullet Power Base and twist it into place. Blast the mixture until it is really smooth (20 or so seconds). **Enjoy!**

Plum Job

Ingredients

1 Cup/Handful of Green Cabbage (40 grams or 1½ oz)
1 Cup/Handful of Fennel (40 grams or 1½ oz)
1 Cup of Plum halves (120 grams or 4 oz)
1 Cup of Radishes (120 grams or 4 oz)
200 ml / 7 fl oz of Half Fat Crème Fraiche

Protein 3g, Fat 31g, Carb 28g, Fibre 6g, 434 Kcals

Preparation

Put all the solid ingredients into the Tall Cup and press them down below the Max Line. Add the fluid base to fill the cup up to the Max Line. Screw the Nutribullet Extractor Blade on to the top of the cup. Invert the cup, press it down into the Nutribullet Power Base and twist it into place. Blast the mixture until it is really smooth (20 or so seconds). **Enjoy!**

Green Pepper Power

Ingredients

1 Cup/Handful of Watercress (40 grams or 1½ oz)
1 Cup/Handful of Bok Choy (40 grams or 1½ oz)
1 Cup of Blackberries (120 grams or 4 oz)
1 Cup of sliced Green Pepper (120 grams or 4 oz)
200 ml / 7 fl oz of Greek Yoghurt

Protein 13g, Fat 20g, Carb 20g, Fibre 9g, 335 Kcals

Preparation

Put all the solid ingredients into the Tall Cup and press them down below the Max Line. Add the fluid base to fill the cup up to the Max Line. Screw the Nutribullet Extractor Blade on to the top of the cup. Invert the cup, press it down into the Nutribullet Power Base and twist it into place. Blast the mixture until it is really smooth (20 or so seconds). **Enjoy!**

Orange Morning

Ingredients

1 Cup/Handful of Red or White Cabbage (40 grams or 1½ oz)
1 Cup/Handful of Mint (40 grams or 1½ oz)
1 Cup of Orange segments (120 grams or 4 oz)
1 Cup of diced Swede (120 grams or 4 oz)
200 ml / 7 fl oz of Hazelnut Milk

Protein 4g, Fat 4g, Carb 26g, Fibre 9g, 179 Kcals

Preparation

Put all the solid ingredients into the Tall Cup and press them down below the Max Line. Add the fluid base to fill the cup up to the Max Line. Screw the Nutribullet Extractor Blade on to the top of the cup. Invert the cup, press it down into the Nutribullet Power Base and twist it into place. Blast the mixture until it is really smooth (20 or so seconds). **Enjoy!**

Spinach loves Cherry

Ingredients

1 Cup/Handful of Broccoli Florets (40 grams or 1½ oz)
1 Cup/Handful of Spinach (40 grams or 1½ oz)
1 Cup of Cherries (stoned) (120 grams or 4 oz)
1 Cup of sliced Yellow Pepper (120 grams or 4 oz)
200 ml / 7 fl oz of Dairy Milk Whole

Protein 11g, Fat 8g, Carb 34g, Fibre 6g, 258 Kcals

Preparation

Put all the solid ingredients into the Tall Cup and press them down below the Max Line. Add the fluid base to fill the cup up to the Max Line. Screw the Nutribullet Extractor Blade on to the top of the cup. Invert the cup, press it down into the Nutribullet Power Base and twist it into place. Blast the mixture until it is really smooth (20 or so seconds). **Enjoy!**

Tangerine needs Tomato

Ingredients

1 Cup/Handful of Spinach (40 grams or 1½ oz)
1 Cup/Handful of Rocket/Arugura Lettuce (40 grams or 1½ oz)
1 Cup of Tangerine slices (120 grams or 4 oz)
1 Cup of sliced Tomato (120 grams or 4 oz)
200 ml / 7 fl oz of Coconut Milk

Protein 4g, Fat 3g, Carb 24g, Fibre 5g, 140 Kcals

Preparation

Put all the solid ingredients into the Tall Cup and press them down below the Max Line. Add the fluid base to fill the cup up to the Max Line. Screw the Nutribullet Extractor Blade on to the top of the cup. Invert the cup, press it down into the Nutribullet Power Base and twist it into place. Blast the mixture until it is really smooth (20 or so seconds). **Enjoy!**

Fennel Fix

Ingredients

1 Cup/Handful of Fennel (40 grams or 1½ oz)
1 Cup/Handful of Bok Choy (40 grams or 1½ oz)
1 Cup of Strawberries (120 grams or 4 oz)
1 Cup of diced Turnip (120 grams or 4 oz)
200 ml / 7 fl oz of Almond Milk (Unsweetened)

Protein 4g, Fat 3g, Carb 15g, Fibre 7g, 115 Kcals

Preparation

Put all the solid ingredients into the Tall Cup and press them down below the Max Line. Add the fluid base to fill the cup up to the Max Line. Screw the Nutribullet Extractor Blade on to the top of the cup. Invert the cup, press it down into the Nutribullet Power Base and twist it into place. Blast the mixture until it is really smooth (20 or so seconds). **Enjoy!**

Broccoli and Mint Seduction

Ingredients

1 Cup/Handful of Broccoli Florets (40 grams or 1½ oz)
1 Cup/Handful of Mint (40 grams or 1½ oz)
1 small Apple (cored) (120 grams or 4 oz)
1 Cup of sliced Red Pepper (120 grams or 4 oz)
200 ml / 7 fl oz of Greek Yoghurt

Protein 12g, Fat 20g, Carb 32g, Fibre 9g, 380 Kcals

Preparation

Put all the solid ingredients into the Tall Cup and press them down below the Max Line. Add the fluid base to fill the cup up to the Max Line. Screw the Nutribullet Extractor Blade on to the top of the cup. Invert the cup, press it down into the Nutribullet Power Base and twist it into place. Blast the mixture until it is really smooth (20 or so seconds). **Enjoy!**

Banana joins Celery

Ingredients

2 Cups/Handfuls of Rocket/Arugura Lettuce (80 grams or 3 oz)
1 small Banana (peeled and sliced) (120 grams or 4 oz)
1 Cup of sliced Celery (120 grams or 4 oz)
200 ml / 7 fl oz of Dairy Milk Whole

Protein 10g, Fat 8g, Carb 37g, Fibre 6g, 265 Kcals

Preparation

Put all the solid ingredients into the Tall Cup and press them down below the Max Line. Add the fluid base to fill the cup up to the Max Line. Screw the Nutribullet Extractor Blade on to the top of the cup. Invert the cup, press it down into the Nutribullet Power Base and twist it into place. Blast the mixture until it is really smooth (20 or so seconds). **Enjoy!**

Peeled Fig and Zucchini Sunshine

Ingredients

1 Cup/Handful of Red or White Cabbage (40 grams or 1½ oz)
1 Cup/Handful of Green Cabbage (40 grams or 1½ oz)
1 Cup of Peeled Figs (120 grams or 4 oz)
1 Cup of sliced Zucchini/Courgette (120 grams or 4 oz)
200 ml / 7 fl oz of Hazelnut Milk

Protein 4g, Fat 4g, Carb 31g, Fibre 7g, 189 Kcals

Preparation

Put all the solid ingredients into the Tall Cup and press them down below the Max Line. Add the fluid base to fill the cup up to the Max Line. Screw the Nutribullet Extractor Blade on to the top of the cup. Invert the cup, press it down into the Nutribullet Power Base and twist it into place. Blast the mixture until it is really smooth (20 or so seconds). **Enjoy!**

Lettuce and Watercress Waistline

Ingredients

1 Cup/Handful of Lettuce Leaves (40 grams or 1½ oz)
1 Cup/Handful of Watercress (40 grams or 1½ oz)
1 Cup of Apricot halves (120 grams or 4 oz)
1 Cup of sliced Red Pepper (120 grams or 4 oz)
200 ml / 7 fl oz of Almond Milk (Unsweetened)

Protein 5g, Fat 3g, Carb 17g, Fibre 7g, 131 Kcals

Preparation

Put all the solid ingredients into the Tall Cup and press them down below the Max Line. Add the fluid base to fill the cup up to the Max Line. Screw the Nutribullet Extractor Blade on to the top of the cup. Invert the cup, press it down into the Nutribullet Power Base and twist it into place. Blast the mixture until it is really smooth (20 or so seconds). **Enjoy!**

Prune and Swede Embrace

Ingredients

1 Cup/Handful of Rocket/Arugura Lettuce (40 grams or 1½ oz)
1 Cup/Handful of Watercress (40 grams or 1½ oz)
1 Cup of Prunes (stoned) (120 grams or 4 oz)
1 Cup of diced Swede (120 grams or 4 oz)
200 ml / 7 fl oz of Half Fat Crème Fraiche

Protein 4g, Fat 32g, Carb 22g, Fibre 6g, 388 Kcals

Preparation

Put all the solid ingredients into the Tall Cup and press them down below the Max Line. Add the fluid base to fill the cup up to the Max Line. Screw the Nutribullet Extractor Blade on to the top of the cup. Invert the cup, press it down into the Nutribullet Power Base and twist it into place. Blast the mixture until it is really smooth (20 or so seconds). **Enjoy!**

Bok Choy Elixir

Ingredients

1 Cup/Handful of Fennel (40 grams or 1½ oz)
1 Cup/Handful of Bok Choy (40 grams or 1½ oz)
1 Cup of Kiwi Fruit slices (120 grams or 4 oz)
1 Cup of sliced Cucumber (120 grams or 4 oz)
200 ml / 7 fl oz of Coconut Milk

Protein 3g, Fat 3g, Carb 23g, Fibre 6g, 145 Kcals

Preparation

Put all the solid ingredients into the Tall Cup and press them down below the Max Line. Add the fluid base to fill the cup up to the Max Line. Screw the Nutribullet Extractor Blade on to the top of the cup. Invert the cup, press it down into the Nutribullet Power Base and twist it into place. Blast the mixture until it is really smooth (20 or so seconds). **Enjoy!**

Yellow Pepper Cocktail

Ingredients

1 Cup/Handful of Mint (40 grams or 1½ oz)
1 Cup/Handful of Red or White Cabbage (40 grams or 1½ oz)
1 Cup of Raspberries (120 grams or 4 oz)
1 Cup of sliced Yellow Pepper (120 grams or 4 oz)
200 ml / 7 fl oz of Water

Protein 5g, Fat 1g, Carb 15g, Fibre 12g, 124 Kcals

Preparation

Put all the solid ingredients into the Tall Cup and press them down below the Max Line. Add the fluid base to fill the cup up to the Max Line. Screw the Nutribullet Extractor Blade on to the top of the cup. Invert the cup, press it down into the Nutribullet Power Base and twist it into place. Blast the mixture until it is really smooth (20 or so seconds). **Enjoy!**

Cranberry and Turnip Treat

Ingredients

1 Cup/Handful of Spinach (40 grams or 1½ oz)
1 Cup/Handful of Broccoli Florets (40 grams or 1½ oz)
1 Cup of Cranberries (120 grams or 4 oz)
1 Cup of diced Turnip (120 grams or 4 oz)
200 ml / 7 fl oz of Water

Protein 4g, Fat 0.6g, Carb 17g, Fibre 10g, 111 Kcals

Preparation

Put all the solid ingredients into the Tall Cup and press them down below the Max Line. Add the fluid base to fill the cup up to the Max Line. Screw the Nutribullet Extractor Blade on to the top of the cup. Invert the cup, press it down into the Nutribullet Power Base and twist it into place. Blast the mixture until it is really smooth (20 or so seconds). **Enjoy!**

Green Cabbage Scene

Ingredients

1 Cup/Handful of Lettuce Leaves (40 grams or 1½ oz)
1 Cup/Handful of Green Cabbage (40 grams or 1½ oz)
1 Cup of Grapefruit segments (120 grams or 4 oz)
1 Cup of Radishes (120 grams or 4 oz)
200 ml / 7 fl oz of Almond Milk (Unsweetened)

Protein 3g, Fat 3g, Carb 13g, Fibre 6g, 100 Kcals

Preparation

Put all the solid ingredients into the Tall Cup and press them down below the Max Line. Add the fluid base to fill the cup up to the Max Line. Screw the Nutribullet Extractor Blade on to the top of the cup. Invert the cup, press it down into the Nutribullet Power Base and twist it into place. Blast the mixture until it is really smooth (20 or so seconds). **Enjoy!**

Rocket in Clementine

Ingredients

1 Cup/Handful of Bok Choy (40 grams or 1½ oz)
1 Cup/Handful of Rocket/Arugura Lettuce (40 grams or 1½ oz)
1 Cup of Clementine slices (120 grams or 4 oz)
1 Cup of sliced Tomato (120 grams or 4 oz)
200 ml / 7 fl oz of Half Fat Crème Fraiche

Protein 3g, Fat 31g, Carb 28g, Fibre 4g, 427 Kcals

Preparation

Put all the solid ingredients into the Tall Cup and press them down below the Max Line. Add the fluid base to fill the cup up to the Max Line. Screw the Nutribullet Extractor Blade on to the top of the cup. Invert the cup, press it down into the Nutribullet Power Base and twist it into place. Blast the mixture until it is really smooth (20 or so seconds). **Enjoy!**

Spinach and Pear Perfection

Ingredients

1 Cup/Handful of Mint (40 grams or 1½ oz)
1 Cup/Handful of Spinach (40 grams or 1½ oz)
1 small Pear (cored) (120 grams or 4 oz)
1 Cup of sliced Carrots (120 grams or 4 oz)
200 ml / 7 fl oz of Greek Yoghurt

Protein 12g, Fat 20g, Carb 36g, Fibre 11g, 394 Kcals

Preparation

Put all the solid ingredients into the Tall Cup and press them down below the Max Line. Add the fluid base to fill the cup up to the Max Line. Screw the Nutribullet Extractor Blade on to the top of the cup. Invert the cup, press it down into the Nutribullet Power Base and twist it into place. Blast the mixture until it is really smooth (20 or so seconds). **Enjoy!**

NOTES

NOTES

NOTES

Printed in Great Britain
by Amazon